THE WICKEDNESS
OF PUBLIC EDUCATION

Come Out of Her My People

Dr. Michael H Yeager

Dr. Michael H Yeager

Copyright © 2021 Dr. Michael H Yeager

All rights reserved.

ISBN: 9781073321377
Imprint: Independently published

DEDICATION

Proverbs 22:6 Train up a child in the way he should go: and when he is old, he will not depart from it.

When we bring children into this world, we are given a grave responsibility. Every child has an eternal soul. The destiny of that soul is within the hands of the parents to a great extent. The public education system is never going to train our children to fulfill the first and greatest commandment.

These articles, teachings, true stories have been rewritten by the discretion of the author in order to make them more relevant to the subject matter. Some of this information has been compiled from different articles from the internet. Acknowledgement and links to these articles where it was feasible have been included!

Dr. Michael H Yeager

CONTENTS

EXHORTATION

Only those who genuinely want to know the truth about public education will most likely read this book. I would like to encourage those who have begun reading this book, to read it to the very end. This book is not written just from one person's perspective but from a broad range of godly believers, educators and parents. You will read not just their opinions but their personal experiences. Please read this book with an open heart and an open mind examining it through the lens of God's will and word.

CHAPTER ONE

PSALM 1:1 BLESSED IS THE MAN THAT WALKETH NOT IN THE COUNSEL OF THE UNGODLY, NOR STANDETH IN THE WAY OF SINNERS, NOR SITTETH IN THE SEAT OF THE SCORNFUL. 2 BUT HIS DELIGHT IS IN THE LAW OF THE LORD; AND IN HIS LAW DOTH HE MEDITATE DAY AND NIGHT. 3 AND HE SHALL BE LIKE A TREE PLANTED BY THE RIVERS OF WATER, THAT BRINGETH FORTH HIS FRUIT IN HIS SEASON; HIS LEAF ALSO SHALL NOT WITHER; AND WHATSOEVER HE DOETH SHALL PROSPER.

JOHN WESLEY'S WARNING ABOUT GOVERNMENT SCHOOLS!

"John Wesley was an English cleric, theologian, and evangelist, who was a leader of a revival movement within the Church of England known as Methodism."(28 June 1703 – 2 March 1791)

"Let it be remembered that I do not speak to the wild, giddy, thoughtless world, but to those that fear God. I ask, then, for what end do you send you children to school? Why? That they may be fit to live in the world? In which world do you mean, — this or the next? Perhaps you thought of this world only; and had forgotten that there is a world to come; yea, and one that will last forever!

Pray take this into your account and send them to such teachers as will always keep it before their eyes. Otherwise, to send them to [a government] school (permit me to speak plainly) is little better than sending them to the devil. At all events, then, send your boys [and girls], if you have any concern for their souls, not to any of the large public schools, (for they are nurseries of all manner of wickedness,) but private school, kept by some pious man, who endeavors to instruct a small number of children in religion and learning together."

A WAKE-UP CALL

This book is not written as an attack upon the public school, or secular, liberal, Colleges. Instead, it is a wake-up call to God's people. To our great shame as believers in Christ, we are losing our next generation by allowing nonbelievers to do that which is meant to be our responsibility.

Proverbs 22:6 Train up a child in the way he should go: and when he is old, he will not depart from it.

When we bring children into this world, we are given a grave responsibility. Every child has an eternal soul. The destiny of that soul is within the hands of the parents to a great extent. The public education system is never going to train our children to fulfill the first and greatest commandment.

THE WICKEDNESS OF PUBLIC EDUCATION

Matthew 22:37 Jesus said unto him, Thou shalt love the Lord thy God with all thy heart, and with all thy soul, and with all thy mind.

This book will explore the many different areas where believers are and have been deceived when it comes to the will of God for their children. It is time for God's people to **REPENT** and to stop sacrificing their children to the devils of this wicked world.

About the Author

Dr. Michael H Yeager has published over 170 books up to the publishing of this book. Pioneered a K to 12 Christian School in the state of Pennsylvania and established a Bible College. He helped to start over 25 churches in the communist-infested part of the Philippines. In addition, he has produced and posted thousands of video Messages on the Internet.

He also has written over 5000 sermon outlines on over 30 different subject matters of the Bible. He has preached over 10,000 times. He has memorized a third of the New Testament! Earned a Ph.D. in Biblical Theology and received a conferred Doctor of Divinity from Life Christian University. The most notable success he has had is that he and his wife have successfully four godly children who are all serving the Lord.

WHY MY CHILDREN NEVER WENT ASTRAY

You might ask why do I have the right to write a book about the wickedness of public education? I experienced it as a little boy up to the time I quit public school when I was 15 years old. A little later in this book, I will share those experiences that negatively impacted my life.

Now, after I was born again, I told the Lord that I would never put any of my children into the hands of the world. I would never let them educate my children because I knew they would take them into darkness and perversion.

Psalm 127:3 Lo, children are an heritage of the Lord: and the fruit of the womb is his reward.4 As arrows are in the hand of a mighty man; so are children of the youth.5 Happy is the man that hath his quiver full of them: they shall not be ashamed, but they shall speak with the enemies in the gate.

Psalm 128:3 Thy wife shall be as a fruitful vine by the sides of thine house: thy children like olive plants round about thy table.4 Behold, that thus shall the man be blessed that feareth the Lord.

Isaiah 8:18 Behold, I and the children whom the Lord hath given me are for signs and for wonders in Israel from the Lord of hosts, which dwelleth in mount Zion.

The old saying is **the proof of the pudding is in the eating**. Jesus said: by their fruits you will know them. I am sharing with you not from a heart of pride but of deep gratitude and appreciation to God for keeping my children. Are my children perfect? No, but thank God the world has never swallowed them up. My three sons and my daughter all work with us in the ministry and are ministers of the gospel. They have been the joy of my life and my heart. If you raise your children properly, they will become your greatest blessing by God's mercy and grace.

Our children were educated in our own private Christian school, and at times we even homeschooled them. When my three sons reached a certain age, I took each one of them under my wings. I set up a desk in my office and had them with me wherever I went. Through the years, they have been right at my side working construction. They have been on missionary journeys with me and preached on the streets of Philadelphia, Baltimore, and numerous towns and cities.

I knew in my heart that if they were to make it to heaven, I must have as much influence upon them as I could. This has paid tremendous dividends up to this present moment. My oldest son is now in his 40s and has been my associate pastor since he was 18 years old.

My other three children are in their 30s. By the spirit of God, my daughter has written over 400 spiritual songs and is teaching thousands of people how to memorize scriptures by putting a tune to them. My second son Daniel has written over 10 Christian fiction books that he is using to reach a lost generation. All my children currently are busy writing books to educate children and to reach a lost generation. The Scripture has been fulfilled and that they are arrows in my quiver to overcome the enemy.

But how did you and your wife do this, brother mike? You see, from the time my children were born, yes, even before they were born while they were still in their mother's womb, they have been listening to the word of God. To this day, if you would go to their houses and walk into their bedrooms late at night or early in the morning, you would hear them listening to the word of God.

My wife and I usually go to sleep listening to God's word. Often, in the morning, we will listen to God's word before we get out of bed. Whenever we went on vacations or trips in the vehicle as a family, we were always listening to the word of God, or some wonderful spiritual stories, like Pilgrim's progress on audiotape. I am one of those who can truly say that children are a blessing from God. But they must be raised in the nurture and admonition of the Lord.

Often, minister's children are the worse because of the pressures and the satanic attacks against them. I am also sorry to say that ministers have often turned their children over to the secular world, whether in their younger years or during their college years. I would have rather died than allow the world to educate my children.

I am now boasting in Jesus Christ about their lives. I have never preached or harped at my children. I never put ridiculous constraints upon them. I never put pressure on them to perform because they were the children of a minister. Yes, we did pray with them. Yes, my wife always had devotions with them daily. We did have them in our private school, never putting them into the public school, and they have been highly active in the Lord's work!

I believe one main reason has been the consistent flow of God's word into their lives, causing them never to go into drugs, sexual promiscuity, or outright immorality. There is still hunger in their hearts for God. Faith has been maintained in their hearts because the word of God has been flowing into them from the time they were conceived in their mother's womb. My wife and I have strived to be an example of loving God, serving God, and obeying God. We have humbled ourselves many times in front of them and admitted and repented whenever we have missed the will of the Lord.

My children have often thanked me for making the mistakes they can learn from and that they do not have to go through the same stupid events.

<hr>

A Sad but True Story

When Pat Put His Children in Public School

Hi Mike, this is what happened to my children in public school. (about 2005)

My eldest son was on fire for God at a young age. He was excited to preach with me at fairs and at retirement homes. He made an overseas missions trip at age 14 and got so on fire for the Lord that the youth leader of my church asked me if it would be acceptable if he paired my son up with the most rebellious kid in the group, as they did outreaches, in the hope of bringing that young man to Christ.

I agreed, and He was a blessing to that young man and the whole youth group. He was homeschooled until the 7th grade. The same year he went to a Christian school. He felt strongly in his heart that God was calling him to play football which was only offered in public school. He asked if he could go and I agreed.

*Pastor Mike: during this time, brother Pat called and asked me what I thought. I told him if it was my son, absolutely I would not let him go to a public school. Having attended public school and being a pastor, I knew the devastating results of many Christians who had gone to public school.

Pats story continues: When he started 9th grade, his ambition was to lead students to Christ. In the beginning, he prayed with other kids at the flagpole and joined a bible study at the school. But after a few months, the evil influences in the school began to pull him away from the Lord and entice him to serve his flesh.

By the next year, he renounced his faith and turned his back on God. He then worked on my daughters and was able to destroy their faith as well. It has been a heartbreak to witness this destruction. But, I do not believe this is the end of the story. I stand on the Word of God and His promise!

Isaiah 49:25
But this is what the Lord says: "Yes, captives will be taken from warriors, and plunder retrieved from the fierce; I will contend with those who contend with you, and your children I will save.

The Establishment of "Common Schools"

The "common school" movement encouraged the creation of public schools for multiple purposes. These purposes have turned out to be nefarious at the best.

In the 1830s, Horace Mann, a Massachusetts legislator and secretary of that state's board of education, began to push for the creation of public schools that would be universally available to all children, free of charge, and funded by the state. In most states it is the landowner who has to carry most of the burden of this responsibility of educating the children.

No state has completely abandoned the use of the property tax as a source of revenue for public schools. Some States have shifted from a reliance on local property tax revenues as a substantial source of funding. In these cases, the state took on a larger role in the administration of the property tax revenues, in essence shifting from local property tax reliance to state property tax oversight. By oversight, I mean that the state sets the tax rates or tax ceilings or floors for local school districts (or parent governments).

Mann and other proponents of "common schools" emphasized that a public investment in education would benefit the whole nation by transforming children into literate, moral, and productive citizens. Actually, what has taken place in public education is that the children have been indoctrinated into embracing big government, and socialistic controls over the population.

Common school advocates emphasized the knowledge, civic, and economic benefits of public schooling. While hiding their nefarious purpose behind the smokescreen of what is best for the children and the nation. They began this evil plan by what seemed to be common sense education.

Schools were to teach the "three R's" (reading, writing, arithmetic), along with other subjects such as history, geography, grammar, and rhetoric. A strong dose of moral instruction (which has all but disappeared) would also be provided to instill civic virtues. Supposedly educating children of the poor and middle classes would prepare them to obtain good jobs, proponents argued, and thereby strengthen the nation's economic position. It turns out they were preparing these young people to become the work ants for the wealthy and prosperous of our nation.

In the book titled: **Rich Dad Poor Dad,** the author reveals the shocking truth that the educational system is set up to keep most people poor. The system is designed to make people nothing but subservience to the upper class.

Proponents of the common school argued that common schools would not truly serve as a unifying force if private schools drew off substantial numbers of students, resources, and parental support from the most advantaged groups. To succeed, a system of common schooling would have to enroll enough children from all social classes, including the most affluent and well-educated families.

This idea met with great resistance from many Americans who did not want to trust their children's education to a bunch of bureaucrats. They were right to be concerned.

Advocates in all reality saw universal education as a means to control the masses. To enslave them to government control and laborers for those who were at the top of the pyramid. There are many articles that are available online to give evidence to these statements.

The Spread of Public Education

The path toward providing universal access to free education (which is not free at all) was gradual and uneven.
Throughout the 19th century, public schools took hold at a faster pace in some communities than in others. Public schools were more common in cities than in rural areas and in the Northeast than in other parts of the country. There were those who in society saw the true disaster that would come based upon the government-controlled school system.

Gradually, more states accepted the entanglement for providing universal public education and even embedded this principle in their state constitutions. However, not until the latter part of the 19th century did public elementary schools become available to all children in nearly all parts of the country. In 1830, about 55% of children aged 5 to 14 were enrolled in public schools; by 1870, this figure had risen to about 78%. High school attendance did not become commonplace until the 20th century. In 1910, just 14% of Americans aged 25 and older had completed government-controlled high school. As recently as 1970, the high school completion rate was only 55%. In 2017, 90% of Americans aged 25 and older had a government-recognized high school degree.

The Shocking Truth of Public Education
by Sam Blumenfeld

Most Americans assume that we've always had public schools, that they came with the Constitution and are an indispensable part of our democratic system. But nothing could be farther from the truth as I discovered when I wrote my book, Is Public Education Necessary? (published in 1981). In writing that book, I wanted to find out why the American people put education in the hands of government so early in their history. I was quite surprised to find that it had nothing to do with economics or the lack of literacy. It was the result of a philosophical change in the minds of the academic elite.

The U.S. Constitution does not mention education anywhere. It was left up to the states, parents, religious denominations, and school proprietors to deal with. True, in the early days of New England, towns were required to maintain common schools supported and controlled by the local citizenry. This had been done to make sure that children learned to read so that they could read the Bible and go on to higher education. But there was much homeschooling, private tutoring, private academies, church schools, and dames' schools for very young children. There were no compulsory school attendance laws and no centralized state control over the curriculum.

This system, or lack of it, produced a highly literate population that could read the Federalist Papers, the King James Version of the Bible, and everything else that was published. All one has to do is read a Farmer's Journal of those early days to realize the high level of literacy that was enjoyed by the general population in America prior to the advent of the public schools.

What changed all of that was the change in the religious views of the intellectual elite centered at Harvard University, which had been founded in 1638 by Calvinists. By 1805, religious liberalism in the form of the Unitarian heresy had become so strong at Harvard, that the Calvinists were expelled. From then on, Unitarianism reigned supreme at America's foremost university, and its influence spread slowly over the rest of the academic world.

The Unitarians no longer believed in salvation through Christ, whom they considered to be a great teacher but not divine. Salvation was now to be attained through an education controlled by the government. They believed that only government could provide the kind of secular, nonsectarian education that could lead to reason-based moral perfectibility. So believed the Unitarians.

The Unitarians also adopted the Prussian form of state-controlled education as their ideal model for America. Through unrelenting propaganda, social fervor, and political action, they enacted laws that formed the foundation of centralized, state-owned, and controlled education throughout America. Compulsory school attendance was then written into the constitutions of many of the new states, thus ensuring the creation and maintenance of a permanent state bureaucracy in control of education. By the 1870s, the public school movement had triumphed, and most private academies went out of business.

Also imported from Europe was the idea of Hegelian statism, the idea that the state was God on earth. This idea emboldened educators to believe that it was the state's duty to mold its children—its "most precious natural resource"—into obedient servants of the state.

Finally, at the turn of the century, the progressives became dominant. They were members of the Protestant academic elite who no longer believed in the religion of their fathers. They put their new faith in science, evolution, and psychology. Science explained the material world, evolution explained the origins of living matter, and psychology permitted man to scientifically study human nature and provided the scientific means to control human beings.

The progressives were also socialists because they had to deal with the problem of evil and decided that the Bible was all wrong about man's innate depravity. They believed that evil was caused by ignorance, poverty, and social injustice, and that the main cause of social injustice was our capitalist system. And so they embarked on a messianic crusade to change America from a religious, capitalist nation into an atheist or humanist socialist nation. They decided that the most effective way to attain their social utopia was through public education. And so, they began their great movement of education reform that changed our public schools into the moral, social, and academic mess they are today.

During the Carter administration, the formation of the U.S.

Department of Education was the fulfillment of a hundred-year dream by educators. With the passage of the Elementary and Secondary Education Act of 1965, they finally gained unlimited access to the U.S. Treasury. It is obvious now to anyone who has studied public education at any depth that the system is taking us toward the New World Order, in which UNESCO will become the world government's Board of Education.

That is why more and more parents are beginning to realize that public schools are not interested in education but in social change and social control. A government education system is basically incompatible with the values of a free society. Eventually, one or the other must go.

https://www.home-school.com/Articles/the-history-of-public-education.php.

CHAPTER TWO

'Stop Pretending Public Schools Aren't Bad'

Tony Perkins (2020)

There have been plenty of issues over the last year and a half where Democrats have had to "bring Joe Biden along." Whether it was the Hyde amendment, socialized medicine, or religious tests, the Democrats had to move several clicks to the Left to meet the party's radical new standard. That was never the case with the LGBT agenda. In fact, you could make the argument that when it comes to things like transgenderism, it's Biden doing the pulling. And his first day behind the Resolute Desk proved it.

A liberal with a cause is concerning. A liberal who believes in that cause is dangerous. Our nation will find that out for itself under this president sooner than many had hoped. The man who said the only way to restore America's soul was "unity, unity" showed how insincere he is about pursuing it hours later when he picked up a pen and declared war on people of faith. But then, it's not like he didn't warn us.

Biden's "day one" agenda, we heard over and over again, would be throwing thousands of years of human gender norms on the trash heap of history. "I will just flat-out change the law," he told one mother. And Wednesday, he kept that promise, flinging open the door to gender-free bathrooms, locker rooms, showers, changing rooms, sports teams, and overnights. It is the "trans-ing" of America, and under this administration, it's only beginning.

The Federalist's Joy Pullmann knew this was coming. Just look at what's already happened. She wrote in a powerful piece that every American should read about what Biden's election means for education. We already had schools keeping students' gender choices a secret. Male coaches are forced to watch naked female students. Schools dishing out hormones and drugs without parents' consent, including dangerous vaccinations! Preschoolers and kindergarteners are subjected to teachers who identify as transgender and twisted sex lessons they don't understand.

"All of this," Joy insists, "will be accelerated under a Biden administration. This is not conjecture. He and his campaign have publicly pledged to do it." His own political history ought to prove to everyone how sincere he is on this gender extremism. The man who outed Barack Obama on same-sex marriage in 2012 has been a true loyalist in the cause, insisting eight years ago -- when most Democrats wouldn't even touch the issue -- that transgenderism is the "civil rights issue of our time."

Now, with the full weight of government and Congress behind him, Biden can make good on his plans -- which is so outrageous it makes the Obama administration look like prudes. He'll punish schools that don't follow his mandate for "putting naked children of both sexes together," Joy explains. He'll punish teachers and children for believing the truth about biology and gender. He'll use schools as 24/7 indoctrination centers for "the Left's depraved views of sexuality that conflict with the views of all major world religions." He'll make sure your freshman daughter has a male college roommate -- and prosecute her if they complain. He'll send girls' sports teams away to meets and let boys sleep in the female rooms.

And if parents think their kids are safe because they're in private religious schools, they've got another thing coming. If the school takes a dime of federal money or participates in something as innocuous as the federal meal program, they'll be ordered to comply as well. As a result, Christian colleges could lose their accreditation, student loan programs, biblical hiring, firing, and application processes.

"The evil consequences will be applied to all religious and reality-based institutions possible over the next generation -- unless Americans refuse to comply with this insane and destructive lie. Of course, any backup from politicians half of us elect would help," but, as Joy and I talked about on "Washington Watch," most of them don't have the spine to push back. Sure, there will be a backlash to Biden's orders, Joy said. But more than likely, Democrats will get away with it. Why? Because:

"Too many Americans are lazy cowards who point fingers about problems instead of doing what it takes to solve them, because solving problems is hard and whining on Facebook is easy. Too many Americans want a nice car, comfy house in the 'right neighborhood,' high school sports nostalgia, and frequent eating out more than they want to protect children from being mind-raped by sweetly smiling kindergarten teachers and gawked at by emotionally disturbed peers and teachers."

This administration will do what Leftists do, which is to use every single pressure point they can possibly find to advance their war on family, sex, and children to win more power. And unfortunately, Joy shook her head; Republicans -- apart from Donald Trump, who showed unique courage on this issue -- "failed to use their power to protect their constituents and do the right thing."

So what can parents do? For starters, they can send a message by pulling their children out of public schools. Every time that happens, the public schools lose money. If you want to get the Left's attention, that's one way. Too many parents are sending their kids off to godless institutions that are undermining the values taught at home -- and then wonder why their young adults are make a 180-degree turn from their faith. What do you expect when you put them in the care of a government system that's hostile to everything you believe in? "It's time for us to stop pretending that public schools aren't as bad as they are."

Also, Joy said, we need churches "to stand up and stop enabling the government to basically turn children into heathens using our tax dollars... Every church should become an institution of education. They could have co-ops or private schools. When America was founded, almost every single educational institution was directly descended from a church." Moms and dads can't fight the culture alone. They need grandparents, aunts, uncles, church communities, and other local organizations to come around them and make it financially possible for their kids to get a solid education, rooted in transcendent truth.

Putting aside all the "rot" in the public schools, Joy pointed out, the reality is, most children are getting a horrible education anyway. On core subjects, the government's schools are woefully inadequate. "The bar has been lowered so much by public education, it doesn't take parents much of an investment in time and energy to give their children an advantage over their peers in today's culture."

As Christians, we can't outsource something as important as our children's education. The race against Biden's agenda has started. It's time to take control now -- before it's too late.

MY SON DANIELS EXPERIENCE IN THE PUBLIC SCHOOL

By Doc Yeager

Looking at the insanity that is going on in the public school system.

Daniel: (2015) I volunteered for three days to help at a public elementary school in San Francisco, California. It was an interesting experience, to say the least but not one that I really wish to repeat.

The first day was probably the most shocking. The teacher I was helping outlined the rules to me. Basic stuff mostly but one stuck out in particular.

It was what the teacher referred to as the **Three Positives to Every One Negative Rule**. Basically, if the teacher needs to correct the child or tell him to stop something, he must first give the children three positive statements or complements before he can give them one correction.

As I was with this male teacher, he stuck to it the entire time I was with him, which was amusing and yet very sad at the same time. In my opinion, it was psychological hogwash that this teacher had to comply with.

Here is one example, a child was scribbling and drawing while he was supposed to be doing math, so the teacher walked up to him and said, that's a nice drawing, the color is interesting, your linework is good, but you need to be working on math.

Needless to this child continued scribbling so the teacher tried again. I can't remember exactly what he said but I just stood there with my mouth open at the idiotic rule as the teacher scrambled to find something positive to say to the disobedient and rebellious child who completely ignored him at least two to three times more.

Afterward, I asked the teacher about possible discipline options for a child who was so obviously not doing what he should be doing, and he basically told me there wasn't much he could do.

Now, this all happened within the first hour of me being with the teacher, and you can probably already see what the day was going to be like for the poor teacher.

I could go into detail, but I'm just going to jump to the result for the sake of time.

There was this one very disruptive child, and over three days that I was there, I watched this boy of nine or ten years old constantly do whatever it took to keep all the attention on him.

In a class of over twenty kids, he dictated everything that happened. I'm sad to say I didn't see very much learning going on either, but there was not much the teacher could do about it. He tried many times to discipline the child; tried to get him to be quiet, tried to get him to settle down, but to no avail.

In fact, the one time, he did go out of his way to correct the child by changing a smiley face underneath the kid's name on a blackboard to a frown. This child started to scream and throw a fit like you could never believe. The teacher was not allowed to punish the child in any way.

This teacher had no choice but to call in the principal. The child was escorted from the room but came back in less than five minutes and was still just as disruptive as ever.

This is when I realized that this one problem child was the lowest possible denominator, and he brought everyone else down to his level. Five the end of the year, everyone's education level was the same as this spoiled rotten child. This also was training the other children how to be in control of the class.

The only children who were being educated were the ones with parents who took their time to tutor their children at home. In my opinion, the whole process has become bizarre, twisted and ungodly. Instead of our children being educated to be successful, they are being corrupted and perverted by psychological babble. This all took place in approximately 2015.

The Danger of Public Education

By Murray N. Rothbard

The key issue in the entire discussion is simply this: shall the parent or the State be the overseer of the child?

An essential feature of human life is that, for many years, the child is relatively helpless, that his powers of providing for himself mature late. Until these powers are fully developed, he cannot act completely for himself as a responsible individual. He must be under tutelage. This tutelage is a complex and difficult task. From infancy of complete dependence and subjection to adults, the child must grow up gradually to the status of an independent adult. The question is under whose guidance and virtual "ownership" the child should be: his parents' or the State's? There is no third or middle ground in this issue. Some party must control, and no one suggests that some individual third party have authority to seize the child and rear it.

It is obvious that the natural state of affairs is for the parents to have charge of the child. The parents are the literal producers of the child, and the child is in the most intimate relationship to them that any people can be to one another. The parents have ties of family affection to the child. The parents are interested in the child as an individual and are the most likely to be interested and familiar with his requirements and personality. Finally, if one believes at all in a free society, where each one owns himself and his own products, it is obvious that his own child, one of his most precious products, also comes under his charge.

The only logical alternative to parental "ownership" of the child is for the State to seize the infant from the parents and rear it completely. To any believer in freedom, this must seem a monstrous step indeed. In the first place, the rights of the parents are wholly violated, their own loving product seized from them to be subjected to the will of strangers. In the second place, the rights of the child are violated, for he grows up in subjection to the unloving hands of the State, with little regard for his individual personality. Furthermore — and this is a most important consideration — for each person to be "educated," to develop his faculties to the fullest, he needs freedom for this development.

We have seen above that freedom from violence is essential to the development of a man's reason and personality. But the State! The State's very being rests on violence, on compulsion. As a matter of fact, the very feature that distinguishes the State from other individuals and groups is that the State has the only (legal) power to use violence. In contrast to all other individuals and organizations, the State issues decrees which must be obeyed at the risk of suffering prison or the electric chair. The child would have to grow up under the wings of an institution resting on violence and restriction. What sort of peaceful development could take place under such auspices?

Furthermore, it is inevitable that the State would impose uniformity on the teaching of charges. Not only is uniformity more congenial to the bureaucratic temper and easier to enforce; this would be almost inevitable where collectivism has supplanted individualism. With collective State ownership of the children replacing individual ownership and rights, it is clear that the collective principle would be enforced in teaching as well. Above all, what would be taught is the doctrine of obedience to the State itself. For tyranny is not really congenial to the spirit of man, who requires freedom for his full development.

Therefore, techniques of inculcating reverence for despotism and other types of "thought control" are bound to emerge. Instead of spontaneity, diversity, and independent men, a race of passive, sheep-like followers of the State would emerge. Since they would be only incompletely developed, they would be only half-alive.

It might be said that no one is contemplating such monstrous measures. Even Communist Russia did not go so far as to impose a "communism of children," even though it did almost everything else to eliminate freedom. The point is, however, that this is the logical goal of the Statists in education. The issue which has been joined in the past and in the present is: shall there be a free society with parental control or a despotism with State control?

We shall see the logical development of the idea of State encroachment and control. America, for example, began, for the most part, with a system of either completely private or with philanthropic schools. Then, in the nineteenth century, the concept of public education changed subtly, until everybody was urged to go to public school, and private schools were accused of being divisive. Finally, the State imposed compulsory education on the people, forcing children to go to public schools or setting up arbitrary standards for private schools. In addition, parental instruction was frowned on. Thus, the State has been warring with parents for control over their children.

Not only has there been a trend toward increased State control, but the effects of this have been worsened by the very system of equality before the law that applies in political life. There has been the growth of a passion for equality in general. The result has been a tendency to regard every child as equal to every other child, deserve equal treatment, and impose complete uniformity in the classroom. Formerly, this had tended to be set at the average level of the class; but this being frustrating to the dullest (who, however, must be kept at the same level as the others, in the name of equality and democracy), the teaching tends more and more to be set at the lowest levels.

We shall see that since the State began to control education, its evident tendency has been more and more to act in such a manner as to promote repression and hindrance of education, rather than the true development of the individual. Its tendency has been for compulsion, for enforced equality at the lowest level, for the watering down of the subject and even the abandonment of all formal teaching, for the inculcation of obedience to the State and to the "group," rather than the development of self-independence, for the deprecation of intellectual subjects. And finally, it is the drive of the State and its minions for power that explains the "modern education" creed of "education of the whole child" and making the school a "slice of life," where the individual plays, adjusts to the group, etc.

THE WICKEDNESS OF PUBLIC EDUCATION

The effect of this, as well as all the other measures, is to repress any tendency for the development of reasoning powers and individual independence; to try to usurp in various ways the "educational" function (apart from formal instruction) of the home and friends, and to try to mold the "whole child" in the desired paths. Thus, "modern education" has abandoned the school functions of formal instruction in favor of molding the total personality both to enforce equality of learning at the level of the least educable, and to usurp the general educational role of home and other influences as much as possible. Since no one will accept outright State "communization" of children, even in Communist Russia, it is obvious that State control has to be achieved more silently and subtly.

For anyone who is interested in the dignity of human life, in the progress and development of the individual in a free society, the choice between parental and State control over the children is clear.

Is there, then, to be no State interference whatever in the relations between parent and child? Suppose that the parents aggress upon and mutilate the child? Are we to permit this? If not, where are we to draw the line? The line can be simply drawn. The State can adhere strictly to the function of defending everyone from the aggressive violence of everyone else. This will include children as well as adults, since children are potential adults and future freemen. Simple failure to "educate," or rather, instruct, is no grounds whatever for interference. The difference between these cases was succinctly put by Herbert Spencer:

No cause for such [state] interposition can be shown until the children's rights have been violated and that their rights are not violated by a neglect of their education [actually, instruction]. For

... what we call rights are merely arbitrary subdivisions of the general liberty to exercise the faculties; that only can be called an infringement of rights that diminishes this liberty — cuts off a previously existing power to pursue the objects of desire.

Now the parent who is careless of a child's education does not do this. The liberty to exercise faculties is left intact. Omitting instruction in no way takes from a child's freedom to do whatsoever it wills in the best way it can, and this freedom is all that equity demands. Every aggression, be it remembered — every infraction of rights — is necessarily active; whilst every neglect, carelessness, omission, is as necessarily passive. Consequently, however wrong the non-performance of a parental duty may be ... it does not amount to a breach of the law of equal freedom and cannot, therefore, be taken cognizance of by the state.1

Excerpted from Education: Free and Compulsory

Murray N. Rothbard (1926–1995) was dean of the Austrian School, founder of modern libertarianism, and academic vice president of the Mises Institute.

IGNORANCE IS NO EXCUSE FOR ALLOWING THE GOVERNMENT TO RAISE YOUR CHILDREN

Ignorance – especially ignorance of God, His Word, and His will for you and your children is one of the most destructive tools of the devil. In times past, the heathen nations of the world were left to languish in superstition, barbaric religious rites, and strange customs, all because of their ignorance of God's purpose for their lives. God wanted to deliver humanity from spiritual ignorance; hence He took it upon Himself to give them His son Jesus Christ that they might know Him, the true God.

However, history records the opposite; despite the provision God made through his son to know Him, there is still widespread ignorance of God's word, will, character and nature.

Hebrews 1:2 Hath in these last days spoken unto us by his Son, whom he hath appointed heir of all things, by whom also he made the worlds;3 Who being the brightness of his glory, and the express image of his person, and upholding all things by the word of his power, when he had by himself purged our sins, sat down on the right hand of the Majesty on high:4 Being made so much better than the angels, as he hath by inheritance obtained a more excellent name than they.

In due time, God brought the Israelites out of the land of Egypt by a mighty hand; just as He promised Abraham saying:

"And he said unto Abram, Know of a surety that thy seed shall be a stranger in a land that is not theirs, and shall serve them; and they shall afflict them four hundred years; And also that nation, whom they shall serve, will I judge: and afterward shall they come out with great substance (Gen 15:13,14)."

God did according to His promise when the time was due; He saved Israel from slavery and started a long exodus with them to bring them away to the land which he promised to give to Abraham and to his descendants.

ABRAHAM COMMANDED HIS CHILDREN

*We need to realize that one of the reasons why God chose

Abraham was because he knew that Abraham would raise his children and his descendants in the ways of God.

Genesis 18:19 For I know him, that he will command his children and his household after him, and they shall keep the way of the LORD, to do justice and judgment; that the LORD may bring upon Abraham that which he hath spoken of him.

When the Israelites in exodus reached the wilderness of Sinai, they camped there. There, the children of Israel corrupted their ways; that is to say, they apostatized by making for themselves a golden calf, bowed down and made sacrifices to it to provoke God to anger. They were to raise their children with the truth of God's word. But they completely failed to obey.

Deuteronomy 11:19 And ye shall teach them your children, speaking of them when thou sittest in thine house, and when thou walkest by the way, when thou liest down, and when thou risest up.20 And thou shalt write them upon the door posts of thine house, and upon thy gates:21 That your days may be multiplied, and the days of your children, in the land which the Lord sware unto your fathers to give them, as the days of heaven upon the earth.

Instead of raising their children in the ways of God they rebelled against the commandment of the Lord and offered their children up to idols as sacrifices.

Leviticus 18:21 - And thou shalt not let any of thy seed pass through the fire to Molech, neither shalt thou profane the name of thy God: I am the LORD.

THE WICKEDNESS OF PUBLIC EDUCATION

Deuteronomy 12:31 - Thou shalt not do so unto the LORD thy God: for every abomination to the LORD, which he hateth, have they done unto their gods; for even their sons and their daughters they have burnt in the fire to their gods.

Leviticus 20:1-5 - And the LORD spake unto Moses, saying, (Read More...)

Ezekiel 16:20-21 - Moreover thou hast taken thy sons and thy daughters, whom thou hast borne unto me, and these hast thou sacrificed unto them to be devoured. Is this of thy whoredoms a small matter, (Read More...)

2 Kings 21:2-6 - And he did that which was evil in the sight of the LORD, after the abominations of the heathen, whom the LORD cast out before the children of Israel. (Read More...)

2 Kings 17:17-18 - And they caused their sons and their daughters to pass through the fire, and used divination and enchantments, and sold themselves to do evil in the sight of the LORD, to provoke him to anger. (Read More...)

Psalms 106:37-38 - Yea, they sacrificed their sons and their daughters unto devils, (Read More...)

Jeremiah 7:30-34 - For the children of Judah have done evil in my sight, saith the LORD: they have set their abominations in the house which is called by my name, to pollute it. (Read More...)

Psalms 139:13 - 127:16 - For thou hast possessed my reins: thou hast covered me in my mother's womb. (Read More...)

Psalms 127:3 - Lo, children are an heritage of the LORD: and the fruit of the womb is his reward.

Jeremiah 7:31 - And they have built the high places of Tophet, which is in the valley of the son of Hinnom, to burn their sons and their daughters in the fire; which I commanded them not, neither came it into my heart.

Ezekiel 16:36-38 - Thus saith the Lord GOD; Because thy filthiness was poured out, and thy nakedness discovered through thy whoredoms with thy lovers, and with all the idols of thy abominations, and by the blood of thy children, which thou didst give unto them;   (Read More...)

Ezekiel 20:31 - For when ye offer your gifts, when ye make your sons to pass through the fire, ye pollute yourselves with all your idols, even unto this day: and shall I be enquired of by you, O house of Israel? As I live, saith the Lord GOD, I will not be enquired of by you.

2 Kings 3:27 - Then he took his eldest son that should have reigned in his stead, and offered him for a burnt offering upon the wall. And there was great indignation against Israel: and they departed from him, and returned to their own land.

Amos 1:13 - Thus saith the LORD; For three transgressions of the children of Ammon, and for four, I will not turn away the punishment thereof; because they have ripped up the women with child of Gilead, that they might enlarge their border:

THE WICKEDNESS OF PUBLIC EDUCATION

Jeremiah 1:5 - Before I formed thee in the belly I knew thee; and before thou camest forth out of the womb I sanctified thee, and I ordained thee a prophet unto the nations.

Deuteronomy 18:10 - There shall not be found among you any one that maketh his son or his daughter to pass through the fire, or that useth divination, or an observer of times, or an enchanter, or a witch,

The Lord was angry with their disobedience, and the punishment of their unbelief and rebellion would die in the wilderness. Therefore, God pronounced that those who were twenty years and younger were to enter the Promised Land. The second generation would be raised under the divine guidance of Moses, Joshua and Caleb with the word of God.

The testimony of the first generation is revealed to us in Psalms 95. **Forty years long was I grieved with this generation, and said, It is a people that do err in their heart, and they have not known my ways: (Psalms 95:10).**

This scripture was re-echoed in **Hebrew 3:10 – Wherefore I was grieved with that generation, and said, They do alway err in their heart; and they have not known my ways.**

By this testimony, " … **they have not known my ways"**, God identified ignorance on the part of the Israelites to be one of the causes of their unfaithfulness and their sin of apostasy. Is it that God did not give his laws and status to Israel? Certainly, he did? How were they still ignorant? The Prophets Isaiah might have the answer; it is written –

And he said, **Go, and tell this people, Hear ye indeed, but understand not; and see ye indeed, but perceive not. (Isaiah 6:9)**

CHAPTER THREE

A WARNING TO OUR GENERATION

Now, here is a very serious warning to our generation.

Hosea 4:6 My people are destroyed for lack of knowledge: because thou hast rejected knowledge, I will also reject thee, that thou shalt be no priest to me: seeing thou hast forgotten the law of thy God, I will also forget thy children.

It is not that knowledge was not available to them, they simply rejected it. I believe we are in the exact same situation in this generation. We have all the Scriptures from Genesis to Revelation. We have the history of humanity and all of their failures as a reminder of what happens to those who forget God.

Ignorance on the part of the

Israelites during the era of the judges

Now from the beginning of the exodus, all those who were twenty years and older, died in the wilderness according to the promise that God gave to them because of their unbelief and rebellion. Only those of the second-generation who came out of Egypt entered the promised land by faith. During those 40 years, the second-generation children were educated on how to live by faith and trust in God.

The remnant represents those below twenty years at the time of the exodus and those born through all their journey in the wilderness. By courageous and fearless faith in God they overcame the enemies of the promised land and possessed it.

The second-generation at that time were those young people. These were the Children who experienced the miracles and wonders of God in Egypt and the wonders of God in the wilderness. They were partakers of Manna, drinking the water out of the rocks that Moses struck. They saw the Red Sea split down the middle, and they walked across on dry land. They saw the face of Moses as it glowed when he brought to them the 10 Commandments.

They experienced the fire by night and the cloud by day for 40 years. When they finally made it to the promised land after the last generation died, they saw the River Jordan heap up like a mighty wall as they walked across the dried-up bed of the river. When they had obeyed God and marched around the walls of Jericho for seven days and then on the seventh day on the seventh time they shouted, and the walls of Jericho fell flat to the ground.

They saw the sun stand still at Joshua's word, and their enemies smitten down with hailstones. No enemy of Canaan could stand

THE WICKEDNESS OF PUBLIC EDUCATION

before them all the days of their life. This generation had been raised in the knowledge, the wisdom, and the understanding of what it meant to walk with God by faith.

But once again, unbelief exploded when Joshua's generation (remnant) was gathered unto their fathers: **and there arose another generation after them, which knew not the LORD, nor yet the works which he had done for Israel. Judges 2:10**

Throughout the era of the judges, the generations of Israelites of that age identified with the description **'a generation which knew not the LORD'**. They were not educated in the reality of a holy and mighty God. They began to be corrupted and polluted with the knowledge of the heathen nations around them. This should cause us to stop and consider the generation we are now living in. Most Christians in this 21st century are utterly ignorant of God's will and the word of God even though we have God's complete word and will.

Since they did not know the Lord, or His will, their hearts were inclined to do evil. The Bible continues to testify against that ignorant generation of Israelites of all the evil things they proceeded to do against the Lord, saying,

"11 And the children of Israel did evil in the sight of the LORD, and served Baalim: 12 And they forsook the LORD God of their fathers, which brought them out of the land of Egypt, and followed other gods, of the gods of the people that were round about them, and bowed themselves unto them, and provoked the LORD to anger. 13 And they forsook the LORD, and served Baal and Ashtaroth". Judges 2:11-13.

Mostly this generation of Israelites which **'knew not the LORD'** lived a life marked with an abundance sins and defeats. They defiled the commandments of God and committing apostasy in the form of idol worship. Because of them, the expression, **'the children of Israel did evil in the sight of the LORD'** was frequently used in the Book of Judges.

Any time the expression was used, it meant that the Israelites had forsaken the Lord and had gone astray after the gods of the heathen nations round about them. They adopted the educational standards and the worship of the gods of Syria, and the gods of Zidon, and the gods of Moab, and the gods of Ammon, and the gods of the Philistines, and forsook the LORD, and did not serve Him.

First, to what extent was that generation ignorant of God? Better said, what does the Bible mean by the saying, "…. **they knew not the Lord"?** Is it that they had never heard of God? Certainly, the name of God and the salvation He brought to Israel was not blotted out of the oral and written history of the children of Israel. Hence hearing, they had heard of God and knew him, at least, by name.

However, there is more to God than merely knowing his name. Knowing God has everything to do with being well acquainted with his word and practicing the obedience thereof; for the word of God is a revelation that reveals the character of God, the nature of God, the statutes of God; etc.

 In short, God reveals Himself through His word. Thus, the phrase **"…. they knew not the Lord"** means they had not educated themselves with the word of God, nor walked in obedience to God's will or word. At the time of this their great ignorance, the word of God available was the Law – the Mosaic Law – also called the Pentateuch.

Pentateuch means simply "five books". In Greek, the Pentateuch (which the Jews called the Torah) includes the books of Genesis, Exodus, Leviticus, Numbers, and Deuteronomy. God had revealed Himself, His will and purposes, His statutes, etc. through the Law which was given through Moses.

If God had made available the Law, then how come they were still ignorant? For the most part, they were ignorant of the Lord because, right from infancy, they were not taught to know the Law and that they must obey it to be blessed of God.

Joshua 1:8 This book of the law shall not depart out of thy mouth; but thou shalt meditate therein day and night, that thou mayest observe to do according to all that is written therein: for then thou shalt make thy way prosperous, and then thou shalt have good success.

Do we not see this to a great extent right now in America and around the world? Has not the body of Christ forfeited their responsibility to raise their children to an ungodly society who has embraced the insanity of evolution and sexual perversion.

WE ARE RESPONSIBLE TO RAISE OUR CHILDREN

For just a little while, we need to look at a famous person in the Bible who forsook the responsibility God had given him to raise his children properly. Of course, there is way more than just one person we can discover in the Scriptures who did this but let us begin with Job.

Ignorance opens the barn door for the devil to

come and steal, kill, and destroy.

Hosea 4:6 My people are destroyed for lack of knowledge: because thou hast rejected knowledge, I will also reject thee, that thou shalt be no priest to me: seeing thou hast forgotten the law of thy God, I will also forget thy children.

We are at war! Satan hates us and wants to destroy us. We must be aware of the devil's devices, weapons, and tactics, because our spiritual life and eternal destiny depend on it. The apostle Paul was well aware of the dangers Satan poses for **Christ**ians. We must follow Paul's example and not be ignorant of Satan's devices (2 Corinthians 2:11). The New International Version and others translate this as Satan's "schemes." This means we must understand the devil's tricks and traps and examine how he uses his key weapons in individually targeted ways to attack each of us. Unfortunately, **Job** did not have access to this knowledge, but we do.

A LOOK AT HEBREWS

In Hebrews 1 it is revealed that in **"time past"** **God** had spoken to the fathers by the prophets, but now He has spoken to us by His Son, **Jesus Christ**. According to *Ephesians 2:20* the Kingdom of **God** is *"built upon the foundation of the apostles and prophets, Jesus Christ himself being the chief corner stone;"* Please notice that in times past **God** spoke specifically to the fathers by the prophets. Now we have a more certain word of prophecy, a deeper revelation, a more precise understanding of the perfect will of our heavenly Father. Why? Because He is going to speak to us in a very clear and dramatic way. If we believe the words, the life, and the example of **Jesus**, this will radically transform our lives forever.

Remember that all the words that had been spoken up to the coming of **Christ** were to prepare us for the coming of **Christ**. The life of **Jesus** is the perfect will of **God** manifested in the flesh. This is the mystery which had been hidden before the foundation of the world. Notice in Hebrews 1:2: "*Hath in these last days spoken unto us by his Son.*" The foundation of my understanding of the voice of **God**, the will of **God**, the purposes of **God**, the plan of **God**, the mission of **God**, and the mysteries of **God**, cannot be discovered in any greater revelation than that of the person of **Jesus Christ**! I cannot emphasize this enough!

THERE IS NO GREATER REVELATION OF GOD'S PERFECT DIVINE WILL, OR VOICE, THAN WHAT WE DISCOVER IN JESUS CHRIST.

John 1:14 And the Word was made flesh, and dwelt among us, (and we beheld his glory, the glory as of the only begotten of the Father,) full of grace and truth.

If you do not understand that **God** is speaking to you very precisely through His Son, **Jesus Christ**, you will end up being mixed up, confused, and led astray just like **Job**. Learning to understand **God** very precisely is only found in **Jesus Christ**: **whom He has appointed Heir of all things, and by whom He made the worlds.** Notice that Hebrews 1:3 boldly declares **Jesus Christ** is the brightness of the Father's glory, the manifestation of the Father's presence, and the express image of His personality. He is like a mirror reflecting the perfect image of the heavenly Father to all of humanity. **Jesus** declared:

John 14:9-10 Jesus saith unto him, Have I been so long time with you, and yet hast thou not known me, Philip? he that hath seen me hath seen the Father; and how sayest thou then, Show us the Father? 10 Believest thou not that I am in the Father, and the Father in me? the words that I speak unto you I speak not of myself: but the Father that dwelleth in me, he doeth the works.

Jesus Christ is the absolute perfect will of the Father revealed to you and me and for our children. The deepest revelation of the Father is only discovered in **Jesus Christ**. Paul, the apostle, commands us to have the mind of **Christ**:

Philippians 2:5-11 Let this mind be in you, which was also in Christ Jesus: 6 Who, being in the form of God, thought it not robbery to be equal with God: 7 But made himself of no reputation, and took upon him the form of a servant, and was made in the likeness of men: 8 And being found in fashion as a man, he humbled himself, and became obedient unto death, even the death of the cross. 9 Wherefore God also hath highly exalted him, and given him a name which is above every name: 10 That at the name of Jesus every knee should bow, of things in heaven, and things in earth, and things under the earth; 11 And that every tongue should confess that Jesus Christ is Lord, to the glory of God the Father.

When we look at **Jesus**, and hear His words, it is the Father we are looking at. The apostle, John, boldly declares in John 1:

John 1:1-3 In the beginning was the Word, and the Word was with God, and the Word was God. 2 The same was in the beginning with God. 3 All things were made by him; and without

him was not any thing made that was made.

The Word made all things. But, what "Word" is it talking about? The written word? Or **Christ**, the Word? It is evident that it is the person, **Christ Jesus**, Emmanuel, **God** is with us!

John 1:14 And the Word was made flesh, and dwelt among us, (and we beheld his glory, the glory as of the only begotten of the Father,) full of grace and truth.

The reality is this: for us to rightly discern the Word of **God** we must know the person of **Christ**, discovered in the four gospels. What do I mean by this statement? When I gave my heart to **Jesus Christ** (on February 18, 1975, at about 3 p.m.) all I had available to me was a little military green Bible. The moment **Christ** came into my heart I picked up that little Bible and began to devour it. The four gospels of **Jesus Christ**: Matthew, Mark, Luke, and John, became my favorite books.

The Four Gospels

It Is Not Just the Preaching of the Cross

Christ and his suffering are so wonderful to me, beyond my comprehension to where it brings me to tears. But there really seems to be blinders on people's eyes at this moment in history. The truth is before us within the New Testament for anyone who is hungry for truth.

Do you not remember when God had them put the brazen serpent upon the pole in the old covenant? Years later, it had to be destroyed (heaven forbid that I am talking about the cross) because it became idolatry. If we do not watch it, we are going to be doing the same thing with the cross. As I say everything must be in balance.

The carnal mind tends to take things out of context or overemphasize one point. We are to eat the whole lamb. Every epistle of the New Testament, and the four Gospels, were perfectly in balance. Everything they proclaimed, even emphasizing how many times words were mentioned, is perfectly in balance.

We cannot improve on it. May the **Lord** give us understanding? I think we have a gospel today with very little **Jesus** in it. Listen to most sermons, and it is very little **Jesus Christ**!

After giving my heart to **Christ**, a divine hunger and thirst for the Word of **God** began to possess me. I practically devoured **Matthew, Mark, Luke,** and **John. Jesus** became my hero in every sense of the word, in every area of my thoughts and daily living. He became my soul reason for getting up every day and going to work, eating, sleeping, and living. I discovered that everything I did was based on a desire of wanting to please Him.

How The Four Gospels Transformed My Life!
1975

When I gave my heart to **Jesus Christ** on February 18, 1975, all I had available was a little military green Bible. Now when **Christ** came into my heart I picked up that little Bible and began to devour it. **Matthew, Mark, Luke,** and **John** the four Gospels of **Jesus Christ,** became my favorite books. I just could not get enough of the beautiful reality of **Jesus**. As I read these four

Gospels, I walked with **Christ** every step of the way. From his birth, through his childhood, his baptism by John when he was 30 years old. As he was led of the Spirit into the wilderness and tempted of the enemy overcoming the devil by boldly declaring **"It is written."**

I spent my first three years as a believer eating and drinking almost nothing but **Jesus** from his four Gospels. Yes, I did read the epistles, and they were wonderful, but nothing captured and captivated my heart as much as the life, the words and the ministry of **Jesus**.

I wept as I read of his sufferings, his crucifixion, and his death. I wept when I saw that the Heavenly Father had to turn his face away from his own Son, because of his love for us. I shouted at his triumphant conquest and victory over every satanic power.

Jesus Christ is the perfect reflection of the Heavenly Father. There is no more perfect revelation of the will of the Father than **Jesus Christ**. Actually, I am extremely happy that I was not influenced by the modern-day church, to a great extent, for the first three years of my salvation. When I eventually came to the lower 48 after living and ministering in Alaska, I was shocked and surprised at what most **Christ**ians believed.

I realize there is a large variety of different interpretations of the Scriptures in many pulpits today. Many of **God**'s people are extremely confused. Many ministers declare insane false doctrines that are so contrary to what I discovered in **Christ**; it is hard for me to believe they even believe what they are teaching. To truly understand **God**, all you must do is look at **Jesus Christ**: His words, deeds, actions, and reactions; His lifestyle and his attitude, mannerism, wonderful character, and the fruit of his life. I can truly say that since I have been born again, I have only had one person who I truly want to be like: His name is **Jesus Christ**.

If the body of **Christ** would simply go back to the four Gospels, and walk with **Jesus** every step of the way, from his birth to his resurrection, to his ascension, much of their confusion would be gone. I believe so many are being deceived by false doctrines and philosophies in the pulpits of America today because they do not know or understand **Jesus Christ**.

Hebrews 13:8, "Jesus Christ the same yesterday, and today, and forever."

In the Old Covenant **God** says: "**I am the Lord and I change not.**" Without truly seeing the Father through the life of **Jesus Christ** and God's word, a believer can easily be led astray by crafty men misusing scriptures. You must see **Jesus** to understand the Old Testament and the Epistles of the New Testament. **Jesus** is the voice of **God**, the absolute perfect will of the Father.

I have heard ministers use the Bible to contradict the teachings of **Jesus Christ**! The reason why false doctrines have been able to take root in the church is that people have not looked to and listened to **Jesus** in the four gospels. If you exalt Christ and His teaching in your mind and heart - above all else – it will be very difficult for the enemy to lead you astray with false teachings and doctrines. Here is an example when it comes to the will of **God** about divine healing.

JOB OPENED THE DOOR TO THE DEVIL BECAUSE HE RAISED HIS CHILDREN WRONG

THE WICKEDNESS OF PUBLIC EDUCATION

If you look in verse four of chapter one of the book of Job, the first thing that we Discover is that his sons and his daughters are living immoral lives. Another translation says: **they would have party time**. The three daughters and the sons came together.

They are all having a big old party. When the devil finally did move on **Job**, it was during the time that his sons and his daughters were having a party. And in chapter one, that is when the devil comes in and destroys and kills his sons and his daughters. They were smack dab out of the will of **God**. And they had been hiding under the coat tail of daddy all those years. You know, the Bible talks about coming underneath someone else's authority. And when you come underneath the authority, you have protection, you have blessings, you have provisions. But when you enter into sin you are out from underneath that righteous authority, and you are on your own.

Job Did This Continually

A lot of our problems is that we do not raise our children according to **God**'s will. Most believers are allowing the secular world to raise their children, and we wonder why we have problems. Job did not raise them to love **God**, serve **God**, **Fear God**, obey **God**. **Job** was a man of integrity. He was a man of honesty. He was a man that **Fear**ed the **Lord**. If you studied the book of Job, you would discover that **Job** had a mingling of **God**ly **Fear** and un**God**ly **Fear**.

Job was a man who ran from evil, but his kids did not. So that is one reason why the protective hedge around Job came down. Many a family have been destroyed because the parents turned their children over to an ungodly system. They did not raise them correctly or discipline them according to the will of **God**.

Job 1:4 And his sons went and feasted in their houses, every one his day; and sent and called for their three sisters to eat and to drink with them.5 And it was so, when the days of their feasting were gone about, that Job sent and sanctified them, and rose up early in the morning, and offered burnt offerings according to the number of them all: for Job said, It may be that my sons have sinned, and cursed God in their hearts. Thus did Job continually.

And if you read down to verse five it says: **then it was so when the days of their feasting were gone about that Job sent and sanctified them and rose early in the morning and offered burnt offerings. According to the number of them all, for Job said, it may be that my sons have sinned and cursed God in their hearts and did Job continually.**

YOU ARE TO TRAIN YOUR CHILDREN

Proverbs 22:6 - Train up a child in the way he should go: and when he is old, he will not depart from it.

Ephesians 6:4 - And, ye fathers, provoke not your children to wrath: but bring them up in the nurture and admonition of the Lord.

Deuteronomy 6:7 - And thou shalt teach them diligently unto thy children, and shalt talk of them when thou sittest in thine house,

and when thou walkest by the way, and when thou liest down, and when thou risest up.

Colossians 3:21 - Fathers, provoke not your children to anger, lest they be discouraged.

Psalms 127:3-5 - Lo, children are an heritage of the LORD: and the fruit of the womb is his reward.   (Read More...)

Psalms 127:3 - Lo, children are an heritage of the LORD: and the fruit of the womb is his reward.

Matthew 19:14 - But Jesus said, Suffer little children, and forbid them not, to come unto me: for of such is the kingdom of heaven.

---

2 Timothy 3:14-17 - But continue thou in the things which thou hast learned and hast been assured of, knowing of whom thou hast learned them;   (Read More...)

Isaiah 54:13 - And all thy children shall be taught of the LORD; and great shall be the peace of thy children.

Proverbs 20:11 - Even a child is known by his doings, whether his work be pure, and whether it be right.

---

3 John 1:4 - I have no greater joy than to hear that my children walk in truth.

CHAPTER FOUR

JOB DID NOT CORRECT HIS CHILDREN

Job did not deal with his children and their sin.

Job 1:4 And his sons went and feasted in their houses, every one his day; and sent and called for their three sisters to eat and to drink with them.5 And it was so, when the days of their feasting were gone about, that Job sent and sanctified them, and rose up early in the morning, and offered burnt offerings according to the number of them all: for Job said, It may be that my sons have sinned, and cursed God in their hearts. Thus did Job continually.

    Job is not the only one who missed **God** in the raising of his children. For example, in the old covenant, we see that Eli, the priest, did not correct his children. If we allow the world to train our children we are making the same mistake!

THE WICKEDNESS OF PUBLIC EDUCATION

1 Samuel 3:11 And the Lord said to Samuel, Behold, I will do a thing in Israel, at which both the ears of every one that heareth it shall tingle.12 In that day I will perform against Eli all things which I have spoken concerning his house: when I begin, I will also make an end.13 For I have told him that I will judge his house for ever for the iniquity which he knoweth; because his sons made themselves vile, and he restrained them not.14 And therefore I have sworn unto the house of Eli, that the iniquity of Eli's house shall not be purged with sacrifice nor offering for ever.

What is amazing is that Samuel the prophet ended up making the same mistake as Eli the high priest. Samuel sons also went astray and did evil in the eyes of the **Lord**. As Samuel ages, he repeats Eli's error and appoints his own sons to succeed him. Like Eli's sons, they turn out to be greedy and corrupt.

1 Samuel 8:1And it came to pass, when Samuel was old, that he made his sons judges over Israel.2 Now the name of his firstborn was Jobl; and the name of his second, Abiah: they were judges in Beersheba.3 And his sons walked not in his ways, but turned aside after lucre, and took bribes, and perverted judgment.

Disappointing sons of great leaders is a recurrent theme in Samuel and Kings. (The tragedy of David's son Absalom occupies most of 2 Samuel chapters 13-19. See "David's Dysfunctional handling of family conflict leads to civil war (2 Samuel 13-19)".

2 Samuel 13:1 And it came to pass after this, that Absalom the son of David had a fair sister, whose name was Tamar; and Amnon the son of David loved her........11 And when she had brought them unto him to eat, he took hold of her, and said unto her, Come lie with me, my sister..........14 Howbeit he

would not hearken unto her voice: but, being stronger than she, forced her, and lay with her. 15 Then Amnon hated her exceedingly; so that the hatred wherewith he hated her was greater than the love wherewith he had loved her. And Amnon said unto her, Arise, be gone.............19 And Tamar put ashes on her head, and rent her garment of divers colours that was on her, and laid her hand on her head, and went on crying..........28 Now Absalom had commanded his servants, saying, Mark ye now when Amnon's heart is merry with wine, and when I say unto you, Smite Amnon; then kill him, Fear not: have not I commanded you? be courageous, and be valiant...29 And the servants of Absalom did unto Amnon as Absalom had commanded. Then all the king's sons arose, and every man gat him up upon his mule, and fled.

You know the rest of the sad story. Later Absalom revolted against David and tried to overthrow his own father as King. If David had disciplined his children from the beginning, none of this tragedy would have ever happened. Most likely, David was not even the one who instructed his sons, but he had hired servants. If you read the book of Proverbs, it seems as if David took more of a leadership position when it came to his son Solomon. The Scriptures declared that in Solomon's young years as a leader of Israel, he loved God.

1 Kings 3:3 And Solomon loved the Lord, walking in the statutes of David his father:

These biblical examples remind us work of parenting is as challenging as every other occupation but far more emotionally intense. No solution is given in the text, but we can observe that Eli, Samuel, and David seem to have given their troubled children many privileges but little paternal involvement or correction. Yet we also know that even the most dedicated parents may face the heartbreak of wayward children.

We must acknowledge that we have missed **God** when it comes to raising our children, and then we can cry out for mercy. It is imperative for us to realize that parenting children is an occupation requiring much patience, correction, prayer, time, training in the Scriptures, and divine love. Ultimately to be a parent—whether our children bring delight, disappointment, or some of both—is to depend on **God**'s grace and mercy and to look to **God** for his divine intervention. One of our deepest comforts is to remember that **God** also experienced a parent's heartbreak for his condemned Son yet overcame all through the power of love.

Why do most people in authority refuse to deal with others' sins under their ministry? I believe it is because the devil tells them you are not perfect. So who are you to deal with this? You have not arrived. You make mistakes. Remember what David did with Bathsheba. David, the king, probably thought to himself: I cannot discipline my children because I used to do what they are doing.

Proverbs 29:15 - The rod and reproof give wisdom: but a child left to himself bringeth his mother to shame.

Proverbs 23:13 - Withhold not correction from the child: for if thou beatest him with the rod, he shall not die.

Proverbs 13:24 - He that spareth his rod hateth his son: but he that loveth him chasteneth him betimes.

Proverbs 29:17 - Correct thy son, and he shall give thee rest; yea, he shall give delight unto thy soul.

Proverbs 22:15 - Foolishness is bound in the heart of a child; but the rod of correction shall drive it far from him.

2 Timothy 3:16 - All scripture is given by inspiration of God, and is profitable for doctrine, for reproof, for correction, for instruction in righteousness:

Proverbs 19:18 - Chasten thy son while there is hope, and let not thy soul spare for his crying.

Proverbs 15:5 - A fool despiseth his father's instruction: but he that regardeth reproof is prudent.

Believed Blood-Covered Unrepented Sin

Instead of dealing with his children's sins, he tried to appease **God** through his sacrifices and good deeds. He got it into his silly head that the blood of the animal sacrifices he was making would appease **God**. I am sure he gave the best of his livestock to the **Lord**, but his motives were wrong. The blood of those animals and his burnt offerings did not wipe away the sins of his children because they were not repentant for what they were doing.

The blood of **Jesus** covers me of all sin, past, present, and future. No, no, no, I say thousand times no. You need to repent and deal with the sin in your life and not just apply the blood thinking it will take care of the sin that you are still involved in. When I say this in you are still involved in, I am talking about sins that you are willingly and knowingly still committing.

JESUS PREACHED REPENT

Matthew 4:17From that time Jesus began to preach, and to say, Repent: for the kingdom of heaven is at hand.

Matthew 9:13But go ye and learn what that meaneth, I will have mercy, and not sacrifice: for I am not come to call the righteous, but sinners to repentance.

Matthew 11:20Then began he to upbraid the cities wherein most of his mighty works were done, because they repented not:

Matthew 11:21Woe unto thee, Chorazin! woe unto thee, Bethsaida! for if the mighty works, which were done in you, had been done in Tyre and Sidon, they would have repented long ago in sackcloth and ashes.

Matthew 12:41The men of Nineveh shall rise in judgment with this generation, and shall condemn it: because they repented at the preaching of Jonas; and, behold, a greater than Jonas is here.

Mark 2:17When Jesus heard it, he saith unto them, They that are whole have no need of the physician, but they that are sick: I came not to call the righteous, but sinners to repentance.

Mark 6:12And they went out, and preached that men should repent.

Luke 5:32I came not to call the righteous, but sinners to repentance.

Luke 13:2 And Jesus answering said unto them, Suppose ye that these Galilaeans were sinners above all the Galilaeans, because they suffered such things?3 I tell you, Nay: but, except ye repent, ye shall all likewise perish.4 Or those eighteen, upon whom the tower in Siloam fell, and slew them, think ye that they were sinners above all men that dwelt in Jerusalem?5 I tell you, Nay: but, except ye repent, ye shall all likewise perish.

Number one, **Job** did not raise his kids, right. **Number two**, he did not deal with their sin.

Job 1:4 And his sons went and feasted in their houses, every one his day; and sent and called for their three sisters to eat and to drink with them.5 And it was so, when the days of their feasting were gone about, that Job sent and sanctified them, and rose up early in the morning, and offered burnt offerings according to the number of them all: for Job said, It may be that my sons have sinned, and cursed God in their hearts. Thus did Job continually.

Job thought the blood would take care of unrepented sin. That the blood would appease **God**. We are not trying to appease **God**, that is not what it is all about. The blood of **Jesus** cleanses the sins of those things that have truly repented.

The Bible says to the believer:**1 John 1:8 IF we say that we have no sin, we deceive ourselves, and the truth is not in us.9 If we confess our sins, he is faithful and just to forgive us our sins, and to cleanse us from all unrighteousness.**

THE WICKEDNESS OF PUBLIC EDUCATION

1 John 1:7But if we walk in the light, as he is in the light, we have fellowship one with another, and the blood of Jesus Christ his Son cleanseth us from all sin.

Matthew 6:15 But if ye forgive not men their trespasses, neither will your Father forgive your trespasses.

The Scriptures prove that a believer's future sins are not forgiven unless he meets the conditions that **God** has laid down within his word. There are many other examples of this throughout the New Testament.

THE WIFE INFLUENCED THE CHILDREN

As I was studying the book of **Job**, I kept asking the **Lord** why did **Job**'s children go so bad? Remember **Job** was a man of integrity, upright, and **Fear**ed **God**. Undoubtedly, he would have trained his children in the same manner. My opinion is that because his marriage was not oneness with serving the **Lord**, it corrupted the children.

Many times, through the years as a pastor (about 45 years of pastoring at the writing of this book) I have seen this nightmare. The husband or the wife is on fire for **God,** and the other one is the complete opposite. In most of these situations, the children follow in the footsteps of the one who is in rebellion to their creator. Remember, a person who is not seeking **God** has a tiny moral compass but their own opinions. Whereas a believer who loves **Christ** strictly adheres to the will of **God** according to the Scriptures.

The flesh always strives against the spirit and the spirit against the flesh. And these are two opposite forces that fight against each other. It is a fight of faith to not allow the flesh to dominate your life. It is very easy to go along with the flesh.

LIFE IS LIKE A BOAT

Life is like a **Man** in a boat on a river. Before Adam sinned, **Man** was floating on a river of life, joy, peace, victory, and intimacy with **God**. After **Man** sinned, he was transferred to a river of death, disease, pain, sorrow and separation from **God**. All of humanity is born on this river of death, and the day will come when every **Man** shall die.

Hebrews 9:27 And as it is appointed unto men once to die, but after this the judgment:

Now when a person gives their heart to **Christ**, they are still in the same boat, on the same river. But, they need to be going up the river, and not flowing with the river. The ultimate destiny of that river is death and judgment.

Every boat is equipped with two oars. **OARS.** *Definition of oar = a long pole with a broad blade at one end used for propelling or steering a boat.*

*One OARS name is FAITH.

THE WICKEDNESS OF PUBLIC EDUCATION

*The other OARS is Obedience.

The **Natural Man** has both **OARS** laying in the bottom of the boat being ignored. They are ignorantly going down the river toward a waterfall that leads to hell, that no **Natural Man** will escape unless they become a **Spiritual Man**. They do not say: I need to turn this boat around and head this boat against the river's flow. They are just floating along, oblivious to their circumstance. This river that all of humanity is upon is called the river of the corrupted nature. To the **Natural Man, it is simply called life as it is**!

Now look a first Corinthians, chapter two, verse number fourteen.

1 Corinthians 2:14 But the natural Man receiveth not the things of the Spirit of God: for they are foolishness unto him: neither can he know them, because they are spiritually discerned.

It does not mean that the **Holy Spirit** does not offer the **Natural Man** salvation, but he does not receive the offer. It does not mean the **Holy Spirit** does not offer him new life, and a better life from scriptures. He just is not interested in what is being offered. Why? **They are foolishness unto him. Neither can he know them because they are spiritually discerned.**

The **Natural Man** is hugely gullible when it comes to the devil's lies but refuses to believe **God** and His Word! Instead, they believe in the wild declarations of wild-eyed experts who have no evidence but are under the control of those who are deceived by the demonic world!

John 8:44 Ye are of your Father the devil, and the lusts of your Father ye will do. He was a murderer from the beginning, and abode not in the truth, because there is no truth in him. When

he speaketh a lie, he speaketh of his own: for he is a liar, and the Father of it.

2 Corinthians 4:4 In whom the God of this world hath blinded the minds of them which believe not, lest the light of the glorious gospel of Christ, who is the image of God, should shine unto them.

#2 The Carnal Man

These are those who have trusted **Jesus Christ** as their savior, being born again, having received everlasting life as a gift from **God**. Those who have not given themselves completely over to the will of **God**.

Romans 8:1 There is therefore now no condemnation to them which are in Christ Jesus, who walk not after the Flesh, but after the Spirit.2 For the law of the Spirit of life in Christ Jesus hath made me free from the law of sin and death.3 For what the law could not do, in that it was weak through the Flesh, God sending his own Son in the likeness of sinful Flesh, and for sin, condemned sin in the Flesh:

The **Carnal Man** can also be likened unto a **Man** in a boat on a river who has two boat **OARS**. *Definition of oar = a long pole with a broad blade at one end used for propelling or steering a boat.*

*One OARS name is FAITH, the other is Obedience!

The **Carnal Man** has both **OARS** attached to the **RIGGER**.

Rigger The triangular shaped metal device that is bolted onto the side of the boat and holds the oars.

The OAR of FAITH to his right side, and the OAR of OBEDIENCE to his left side.

To be born again the believer must have exercised both faith and obedience.

Romans 10:9That if thou shalt confess with thy mouth the Lord Jesus, and shalt believe in thine heart that God hath raised him from the dead, thou shalt be saved.:10For with the heart Man believeth unto righteousness; and with the mouth confession is made unto salvation.

Now, this is not the end of their salvation, it is simply the beginning. They are born again by faith and obedience, by the incorruptible seed of **God**'s Word. But until the day they breathed their last breath they must continue to use the oars of faith and obedience. This must be a faith that produces obedience to the will of their king. One hand is upon the oar of faith, and the other hand is upon the oar of obedience.

Colossians 1:23 If ye continue in the faith grounded and settled, and be not moved away from the hope of the gospel, which ye have heard, and which was preached to every creature which is under heaven; whereof I Paul am made a minister;

James 2:17Even so faith, if it hath not works, is dead, being alone.

James 2:20But wilt thou know, O vain Man, that faith without works is dead?

James 2:26For as the body without the Spirit is dead, so faith without works is dead also.

Now, we could easily change the Word obedience to the Word works. I have written a book entitled: **Works the Evidence of Salvation**. In This Book I Share the Fact That There Are the Works of the **Flesh**, the Works of the **Spirit**, and the Works of Faith. Over 200 times, the word works is used in the New Testament, and 99% of the time they are considered good works, necessary works, required works that come from a heart that is in love with **Christ**, and obedient to **God**'s will.

Hebrews 5:9And being made perfect, he became the author of eternal salvation unto all them that obey him;

Both oars must be pulled with equal force and in a consistent manner for the boat to go against the river's current successfully. If you pull on one oar and ignore the other oar you will go in circles but continue to go down the river towards the waterfall of death. Therefore, the boat does not make any headway in your walk with **God**. You simply keep going around and around in a circle with very little **Spiritual** advancement or growth. It is like a dog that is chasing its tail, around and around and around in a circle.

This born-again person is still ignorantly going down the river even as the natural **Man** is, toward a waterfall that leads to hell. There is no escape, unless this person repents for being **Carnally Minded** and becomes a **Spiritual Man**. But, unfortunately, most of these carnally minded people are completely oblivious to their true **Spiritual** condition.

Revelation 3:15 I know thy works, that thou art neither cold nor hot: I would thou wert cold or hot.16 So then because thou art lukewarm, and neither cold nor hot, I will spue thee out of my mouth.17 Because thou sayest, I am rich, and increased with

goods, and have need of nothing; and knowest not that thou art wretched, and miserable, and poor, and blind, and naked:

---

1 Samuel 23:2 The Spirit of the Lord spake by me, and his Word was in my tongue.

*It is only when believers are carnally minded that they will turn the children over to the secular world for their education. This simply means that they are not operating in the mind of Christ. Remember, God commands us to teach our children in the ways of God.

Deuteronomy 6:6 And these words, which I command thee this day, shall be in thine heart:7 And thou shalt teach them diligently unto thy children, and shalt talk of them when thou sittest in thine house, and when thou walkest by the way, and when thou liest down, and when thou risest up.

Deuteronomy 32:46 And he said unto them, Set your hearts unto all the words which I testify among you this day, which ye shall command your children to observe to do, all the words of this law.

Let Us Continue with Being Ignorant Pertaining to God's Will and Word for Your Children

When there arose another generation after them, which knew not the LORD, nor yet the works which he had done for Israel' is viewed in the light of the commandments God gave to Israel in the

Books of Moses, many questions pop up. Things should not have turned out the way they did because when God gave His commandment and His statutes to the children of Israel, He added yet another commandment to conclude, which is the commandment of education; saying,

6And these words, which I command thee this day, shall be in thine heart: 7 And thou shalt teach them diligently unto thy children, and shalt talk of them when thou sittest in thine house, and when thou walkest by the way, and when thou liest down, and when thou risest up. (Deuteronomy 6:6,7). Also, Deuteronomy 11:19-20

The fact that it is written, ".. and there arose another generation after them, which knew not the LORD, nor yet the works which he had done for Israel" gives us proof that the remnant of the exodus who were the immediate parents of this ignorant generation did not take it diligently upon themselves to educate their children in the word of God as God commanded them, neither did they expound to them the mighty works God did for Israel's salvation in Egypt and in the wilderness wherein they sojourn for forty years. Many years later, God inspired King Solomon to write to emphasize what He said in Deuteronomy 6:6-7 and Deuteronomy 11:19-20.

Solomon wrote:

Train up a child in the way he should go: and when he is old, he will not depart from it. Proverb 22:6

If only the remnant had kept the command of God to teach their children the word of God – the Law of Moses, the story would have been otherwise: there would not have been mass ignorance, leading to mass apostasy. Never would have all the tragedies transpired among the Israelites.

Many years after the ignorance that caused sin and apostasy in the pagers of the judges, the Lord complained once again of the ignorance in the days of Hosea in the ages when kings ruled over Israel. Once again sin and all manner of lawlessness had consumed the land; and the Lord showed His displeasure, mentioning ignorance of His word to be the chief architect of the sins of the Israelites. The prophet Hosea wrote –

1Hear the word of the LORD, ye children of Israel: for the LORD hath a controversy with the inhabitants of the land, because there is no truth, nor mercy, nor knowledge of God in the land. 2 By swearing, and lying, and killing, and stealing, and committing adultery, they break out, and blood toucheth blood. 3 Therefore shall the land mourn, and every one that dwelleth therein shall languish, with the beasts of the field, and with the fowls of heaven; yea, the fishes of the sea also shall be taken away. ….. 6 My people are destroyed for lack of knowledge: because thou hast rejected knowledge, I will also reject thee, that thou shalt be no priest to me: seeing thou hast forgotten the law of thy God, I will also forget thy children. (Hosea 4:1-6)

.

CHAPTER FIVE

Ignorance In the Christian Age

Never has ignorance been as destructive as it has been in this dispensation of Christianity. From the beginning of Christianity and the church, there was no denomination because the body of Christ was one. Along the line, the church in Rome, the capital city of the Roman Empire, emerged and set itself up as the head of the church, which later evolved into a denomination called the Roman Catholic Church. The church gained more power and influence through the Roman political system, and it became very powerful and well resourced.

In process of time, the Roman Catholic Church became a religiopolitical organization that sought after absolute power. The leaders of the Catholic Church, to reduce their members to nothing more than dummies who can be easily manipulated, exploited, and misled, resorted to using the most effective weapon, ignorance of the word of God. Therefore, the Catholic Church prohibited and criminalized the reading of the Bible, such that if you were found with any sheet of the biblical text, you would be condemned to death by burning. And many Christians of that time perished in flames.

The Pope, bishops, priests, and nuns filled the people's minds with superstitions and threats of eternal punishments for not submitting to hierarchy. Purgatory was created to strip the people of what little money they had. They were also taught that if they were to read the Bible, devils would come this to their souls. That only the religious hierarchy had divine revelation to understand Scriptures.

Having successfully led the masses of its congregation into ignorance of the word of God, the leaders of the Catholic Church invented many false doctrines such as the worship of Mary, the worship of statues, praying to saints, purgatory, transubstantiation, etc. They forced these doctrines into the hearts and minds of its vast congregation to accept these doctrinal lies.

For many years, nobody dared to challenge these false doctrines because the congregation was ignorant of the word of God, rendering them powerless to challenge any false doctrine and deception. Therefore, the Catholic Church led the masses into apostasy. For the most part, these masses did not know that they were apostates. More so, the Catholic Church preyed on the ignorance of its vast congregation to make a fortune for the papacy by selling indulgences, etc.

God stepped in and raised men like Wycliffe, Martin Luther, etc., who used to be Catholics and set them against the Roman Catholic Church. These men managed to translate the Bible, recopied and or print the Bible in many languages, and made it available to the people to read.

True Believers Began to Break Away from the Corrupt Church Institution

Luther broadened his position to include widespread reforms. In his Address to the Christian Nobility of the German Nation (1520), he supported the new nationalism by advocating German control of German ecclesiastical matters. He appealed to the German princes to help effect the reformation in Germany. He attacked the claim of the papacy of authority over secular rulers. He denied that the pope was the final interpreter of Scripture, enunciating the doctrine of the priesthood of all believers.

He assailed the church's corruption and attacked usury and commercialism, recommending a return to a primitive agrarian society. Catholic theologians were further aroused with the publication of The Babylonian Captivity of the Church, in which Luther, in an uncompromising attack on the papacy, denied the authority of the priesthood to mediate between the individual and God and rejected the sacraments except as aids to faith.

He followed this work with a tract entitled The Freedom of a Christian Man. in which he reiterated his doctrine of justification by faith in Christ alone and presented a new ideal of piety—that of the Christian man, free in conscience by virtue of faith and charged with the duty of conducting himself properly in a Christian brotherhood.

We Need a New Reformation from The Public Education System of the World

THE WICKEDNESS OF PUBLIC EDUCATION

In our modern society, effects of ignorance of the word of God once again. Thank God that Bibles are being made available in many versions and in many languages throughout the world. However, though Bibles are easily now available, many Christians are Bible ignorant – ignorant because they hardly make time to read the Bible, which many faithful Christians have fought and died for. Ignorance of the word of God is still as prevalent as it used to be in time pass and one of the main effects of this ignorance is the body of Christ sending their children to the secular world for their education. Not only are the adults ignorant of the truth, but their children are also greatly influenced by their lack of biblical knowledge.

Ignorance of the word of God is making our children to become either gullible or unbelieving. The ignorance of our children have caused them to become gullible to the point of embracing any philosophy, false doctrine and deceptive ideology which contradicts Bible teachings, leading to their apostasy.

In a situation where the ignorant Christian tries to avoid being gullible by hardening his heart to reject whatever that is preached, once again, he shall do himself no good because, in that attempt to reject false teachings, he shall reject the true teachings as well. Therefore, whether an ignorant Christian becomes gullible or unbelieving, apostasy is not far from him. However, if he studies the Bible, then and only then shall this person be able to discern the truth from the false and then walk in the truth to preserve their salvation.

It is clearly stated in Hosea 4:6 that God rejects those who are ignorant of His word –

'because thou hast rejected knowledge, I will also reject thee,

that thou shalt be no priest to me: seeing thou hast forgotten the law of thy God, I will also forget thy children (Hosea 4:6).'

Any Christian who does not find time to study the word of God is in danger of being rejected by God. Notice most believers find time to do things relevant to them in their lives, such as eating, working, hanging out with friends, etc.

If a professing Christian finds time for other things but does not find time to study the Bible, then you can tell that they do not count the word of God among the relevant things in their life. And if God's word is not relevant to them, then God Himself is of little or no value to them. No wonder such a Christian risks being rejected by God – because he first rejected to know God by not studying His word.

Ignorance of the word of God makes a Christian get along with certain sinful habits that ruin his relationship with God into apostasy. The Bible says, **"Thy word have I hid in mine heart, that I might not sin against thee (Psalm 119:9-11)."** For a Christian to effectively overcome habitual sins in his life, he is required to study the word of God by heart. Ignorance of the word of God will corrupt the church and make Christians habitually sinful as we see in Hosea 4:1-6.

The Bible provides God's answers and solutions to every problem. However, when a Christian fails to study the Bible, resulting in his ignorance of the word of God, such Christians confide in and chase after certain so-called men of God who are nothing more than wolves in sheep's skin, who deceive, abuse, and exploit them to enrich themselves. Such ignorant Christians who fake men of God exploit often become demoralized and lose confidence in Christianity and backslide from the faith.

THE WICKEDNESS OF PUBLIC EDUCATION

These types of Christians have turned their children over to a secular system that completely corrupts and contaminates their offspring's minds and souls. Modern education in America promotes evolution, homosexuality, lesbianism, sex before marriage, transgenderism, the black arts …etc. all of which are condemned by God's word.

Galatians 5:19 Now the works of the flesh are manifest, which are these; Adultery, fornication, uncleanness, lasciviousness,20 Idolatry, witchcraft, hatred, variance, emulations, wrath, strife, seditions, heresies,20 Idolatry, witchcraft, hatred, variance, emulations, wrath, strife, seditions, heresies,21 Envyings, murders, drunkenness, revellings, and such like: of the which I tell you before, as I have also told you in time past, that they which do such things shall not inherit the kingdom of God.

Conclusion

Today, the knowledge of God is all around us, available for both young and old. In addition, we have more Bibles printed in many versions and in many languages to aid our understanding. The Bible can be bought in print in the book shop, downloaded free of charge, or read online. It is also available as an app to read or listen to on your phones.

There are many other options other than public education when it comes to our children. Abeka has a wonderful video school for children from K to 12. Abeka has done the painstaking prep so you can start off running in the right direction, at a good pace, from day one. In lesson plans and teacher editions, you'll find Carefully

Crafted Content—suggested overall plans by week, month, and year. Suggested steps are laid out for you each day.

The Christians of this generation have no excuse to be sending their children to the secular world for their education. On the day of judgment, we will all give an account of the precious lives that God had put into our hands. If we have turned our children over to the world, we need to cry out to God for mercy and grace to help us to repent of this evil that we have committed.

HOMESCHOOLING

The Truth Is Out - We Do not Need the Public School System by Matt Walsh

"Homeschooling families, which included roughly 3 percent of school-age children in the United States in 2016, have lots of different reasons for wanting to educate their own kids. But they're united in a common assessment: They want out of the traditional system. The question is whether COVID-19 will cause a temporary bump in homeschooling as parents' piece together their days during the pandemic or mark a permanent inflection point in education that continues long after the virus has been controlled. As a result, some families may find that they want to exit the system for good."

The data seems to bear this out. A Gallup poll released last week finds that 1 in 10 families with school-aged children are now homeschooling. That means the number of homeschoolers in America has doubled in just one year. Granted, a portion of these families may return to the public school ranks once the lockdowns and mask policies end (if they do end any time this century), but there is reason to think that, as The Atlantic says, the change may be lasting.

After all, these are families who have unenrolled and severed ties from the school system altogether. In some parts of the country, the number of parents who have taken that step is even more staggering. Texas, for example, has seen a 400 percent increase in parents withdrawing from the public school system, which mirrors pretty closely the reported 300 percent increase in traffic to homeschool.com, an online community for homeschoolers.

The trend towards homeschooling has been given a significant shot of adrenaline recently, but it didn't begin with the pandemic. Over the last two decades, the size of the homeschooling community had already doubled even before the lockdowns began. What was once considered a fringe movement for Christian fundamentalists on one side of the political divide and hippy granola-crunchers on the other, has been increasingly embraced as a possibility for people of all ideological persuasions.

What makes this moment so significant is that the lockdowns have broken the final barrier that prevented many parents from exploring the homeschooling route. That barrier was psychological more than anything. It was the belief that public schools do something special that the average parent cannot emulate or improve upon. Even by people who are otherwise skeptical of government control, it was thought that parents teaching their own children is somehow disordered or weird or backward. We need the school system, it was thought. Education is the system's thing, its speciality. Parents do not have the ability or resources to take its place.

That was always a facade. In fact, parents are the primary

educators of a child, whether they accept that role officially or not. There is nothing the school system does that a parent cannot do. There is no role the school system is better suited to fill. The most natural and, for the child, healthiest, choice is to be taught full time by parents who know them, love them, understand them, and can meet their specific needs. If a large-scale, government-controlled education has any role, it should be a backup, a Plan B (or maybe C or D), not as the automatic, default option.

It is not as though the public school system has been a rousing success up to this point. Headlines this week tell us that young people today have a "shocking" lack of knowledge about the Holocaust. Over half of the respondents in a recent survey did not know that 6 million Jews died in the genocide, and 1 in 10 could not recall ever hearing the word "Holocaust" in their lives.

None of this is shocking. For years, polls and surveys have shown that Americans have a very tenuous grasp of basic subjects like history, science, and civics. A few years ago, a survey discovered that only about 30 percent of Americans could pass a citizenship test. Less than 30 percent could identify the 13 original colonies or one thing Benjamin Franklin was famous for. Almost 40 percent thought he was famous for inventing the lightbulb.

Another study reveals that 1 in 5 Americans cannot name a branch of government. A survey released by the American Council of Trustees and Alumni in 2015 showed that half of the Americans couldn't say when the Civil War was fought. In science, a Pew study finds that just 39 percent of Americans have a high level of scientific knowledge, with 29 percent having little knowledge and everyone else falling somewhere in the mediocre middle.

The media likes to trumpet headlines like these, showing that many Americans are embarrassingly ignorant, but they don't like to connect the dots and draw the obvious conclusion: our education system is an abysmal failure. Indeed, ours is an education system that produces citizens who cannot pass a citizenship test. What more needs to be said?

Of course, we must stipulate that the education system has failed to do what it should be trying to do: equip new generations with the strong base of knowledge and critical thinking skills they will need to be well rounded, well adjusted contributing members of society. On the other hand, it has not failed to do what it has tried to do, which is to indoctrinate new generations into the religion of leftism. The rioters terrorizing our cities, screaming about the imaginary bogeyman of "systemic racism," illustrate at once both sides of this dichotomy.

Public schools simply do not deserve the faith we have had in them, nor have they earned the credit we have often given them. They also do not deserve to be seen as inevitable or necessary. And the school system itself has now admitted as much. By shutting down suddenly, for months on end, and even protesting to ensure that it can remain shut for longer, insisting that it is not an essential service like Walmart or the local liquor store, the school system has let the truth slip: we don't actually need it. Society can function without it. There is nothing it is doing that can't be done at home.

Parents are discovering this, too. They are trying their hand at educating their own children — which is something they were already doing, and all parents already do, whether in official capacity or not — and many are discovering that it's not so hard as they thought. Let's hope even more parents have this revelation and that the government school system is rendered finally obsolete and superfluous. That would be one good thing — one extremely good thing — to come out of this godforsaken year.

Get Your Kids Out of Public School

By Inez Feltscher Stepman

This is the Right's greatest opportunity in decades. Will we take it? We are standing on the precipice of the biggest education revolution in generations.

As schools refuse at union behest to reopen full-time instruction in the fall, parents are flooding into alternative options like homeschooling and pandemic "pods." For the first time in modern political memory, there is likely to be an exodus from public schools.

It will not just be the worst-served in poorer neighborhoods to whom most school choice programs are geared, that leave. It will also be middle-class and wealthier families. This presents the biggest opportunity for domestic victory the Right has had in 70 years—if the Republican Party does not squander it.

William F. Buckley, Jr. may have started the conservative lament about the direction of higher education and academia in 1951, but the Right has only recently woken up to the political dangers of the elementary and secondary system. Perhaps this is because, in many ways, the common school system first implemented in the 19th century has, in the past, been an Americanizing, patriotic, and assimilatory institution.

But as it has done to so many institutions in American life, the Left's long march has turned public school's purpose upside down and inside out. Far from inculcating Reagan's "informed patriotism," today's public schools now teach young citizens an outsized vision of America's faults and a twisted, false view of her remarkable strengths.

While textbook information is proprietary, Howard Zinn's A People's History has long been a staple of high school classrooms, now bolstered by the 4,500 (at minimum) schools that have adopted the 1619 Project curriculum—a curriculum even the Project's author now acknowledges is not factual history, but anti-American polemic.

There's an inverse relationship between civic knowledge and the now-fashionable opinions that America is a racist and sexist country. For example, among people under 45, only one in five can pass the elementary U.S. citizenship exam given to naturalized immigrants. But half of that generation are convinced that America is a racist country and 40% disagree that we should be proud of our history.

There can be little doubt that the effect of public schooling today is far from its original purpose of forming citizens capable of living in a self-governing republic. But for decades, despite a robust private school sector, two million homeschoolers, and dozens of limited school choice programs, public school has remained the default option for 90% of American students. That may be about to change.

The Catastrophe of Remote Learning

With a self-defeating assist from teachers' unions, the pandemic is transforming our education landscape beyond all recognition. Parenting Facebook groups and other online forums are currently being overrun by families desperate to get a handle on what learning at home in a "pod" might entail. Overnight, gathering a handful to a dozen students into a "co-quarantined" teaching or tutoring group has become the hottest new trend in education.

Homeschooling and micro-school parents are finding themselves inundated with questions from friends who had never considered those options before. So many are notifying states of their intentions to withdraw from public schools that government servers, unused to the strain, are crashing. Agencies previously dedicated to the placement of au pairs and nannies are capitalizing on the madness and have switched to matching tutors and teachers with families.

Until enrollment counts in the fall are taken, we won't know for sure the extent of the exodus. But it will almost certainly dwarf average figures. For example, in Montgomery County, Maryland, local parents have heard that instead of an expected enrollment of 2500, as few as 300 students had signed up for their local public school as of early August.

Why is this happening? After struggling through the spring, parents know what districts refuse to acknowledge: distance learning has been an utter disaster. A majority of districts never actually implemented live online instruction and instead saddled parents with a frustrating combination of homework and multiplying digital platforms.

And that was in the better schools; in already-struggling places like Chicago, almost half of the city's teachers did not even bother to log in to the district's learning platforms at least three times a week. So while families limped across the finish line in the initial months of the pandemic, the prospect of beginning another year this way seems to many not just inadvisable but impossible.

THE WICKEDNESS OF PUBLIC EDUCATION

The push to reopen schools does not stem from downplaying or disbelief about the effects of the virus: to the contrary, polls consistently show high levels of anxiety about the safety of students and teachers. If parents felt that schools were negotiating with them in good faith and preparing to deliver a better form of hybrid instruction in the fall, we might not have seen the mad scramble to exit the system.

But instead of working with parents, teachers' unions and districts have chosen this moment to fully reveal how low students and families are on their list of priorities with hysterical hyperbole and outrageous non-health-related demands.

The Unions Have Overplayed Their Hands

First, of course, there's the request for more money from Washington. Unions want $245 billion—more than three times the normal annual federal expenditure—to reopen, despite the fact that funds from the first bailout in the CARES Act mostly have yet to be put to good use. Americans, who consistently and vastly underestimate how much the country spends on education and who have largely bought the Left's lie that schools are underfunded, might have swallowed that one.

But in cities across the country, unions overplayed their hand. In Los Angeles they demanded that a moratorium be placed on charter schools and that the police departments be defunded before schools could open. In-state legislatures across the country, unions lobbied to restrict families from switching to already-operating virtual charter schools accustomed to providing online instruction. A coalition of ten teachers' unions across the country and the Democratic Socialists of America put together a list of political demands for reopening that included banning private school choice, testing, and police in schools.

In places where local authorities initially determined it was safe to open schools, union objections have forced last-minute reversals. For example, in Washington, D.C., unions lined up body bags outside school system offices to show their displeasure with a potential part-time reopening; Washington, D.C. public schools, will now be virtual-only through fall.

Furthermore, unions have been in a desperate bid to foreclose other possibilities for parents. As early as March, they were frantically lobbying state legislatures in a bid to control what they seem to view as their captive market share of families, regardless of the quality of services offered. In response to lobbying from unions in Oregon, the state stopped 1,600 students from transferring to a single virtual charter school network. Similar arrangements were passed in Pennsylvania.

And it's not just their public competition they want to put on ice. In the aforementioned Montgomery County, the municipality initially tried to force private schools to close in fall alongside public schools, a move that resulted in a huge outcry and an appeal to the governor that was eventually honored.

Union and district representatives have been relentlessly encouraging parents to avoid homeschooling or learning pods for the sake of "equity," ignoring that shoddy distance learning also widens education gaps. Even more blatantly self-serving is their demand that parents lie to the state and enroll their children for the funds even if they plan to provide alternative learning environments.

The message from unions and district schools to struggling parents during this difficult time cannot be described as anything but tone-deaf. Many—perhaps millions—of families are getting a hard wake-up call that the current public school system places the needs of their children last while advancing nakedly partisan self-interest. "We don't owe you an education for your child," schools are indirectly telling parents. "But you owe us your tax dollars."

Seize the Day

Unions clearly think parents will tolerate being dictated to, hemmed in, and left bereft of any options other than the shoddy distance learning they experienced back in spring; I do not.

Conservatives should step directly into this opening. Suppose parents are being asked to shoulder the duties of educating their children. In that case, the tax dollars allocated for that purpose should flow directly to them to use for learning pods, private school, homeschooling equipment and curricula, tutors, or any other educational purpose they see fit.

This policy solution is not novel. Education savings accounts, which allow exactly the type of flexible use of state education funds that families so desperately need in the coming months, are already in operation in five states and receive extremely high satisfaction ratings from those who utilize them. As chronicled by Bill Mattox of the James Madison Institute, they've even been used in Florida to fund micro-schools—that is, podding—for years.

Providing families with a portion of the state funds that currently flow directly to districts, whether they're serving families or not, would allow parents of all income levels to hire teachers for small-group, in-person learning. This would alleviate both fears about risk from the virus and some of the equity concerns now raised by unions and the New York Times.

Frankly, rarely, circumstances and policy solutions fit so seamlessly together.

Unfortunately, outside of a few presidential tweets about school reopening, the Republican Party's response has been muted. Senator Rand Paul put his fellow caucus members on notice for considering a $100 billion bailout for public schools, even as they refuse to reopen. He recently introduced legislation proposing to reroute federal education funds (about ten percent of education funding overall) to families. Donald Trump and his surrogates continue to help the cause of school choice from the bully pulpit, and some states like South Carolina, Oklahoma and New Hampshire have redirected aid funds directly to families.

While welcome, these limited and temporary programs are weak sauce considering that the Right has been on its cultural heels for decades, grasping at new ways to make arguments in favor of the American system and way of life to a generation that increasingly, thanks to the public school system and academia, knows little about it other than that it's evil.

The Republican Party and the Right face a vitally important choice in the next several weeks: back parents with funds to support alternative arrangements like pods and seize the offensive against one of the Left's most crucial cultural assets, or patch through some temporary Band-Aids in the hopes that we can all go "back to normal" after the immediate threat has passed. If they choose the latter, the normal we return to—while blessedly happier in certain ways than life in the age of COVID-19—will nevertheless be a return to more decades of culture war losses that the country cannot afford.

Inez Feltscher Stepman is a 2018 Lincoln Fellow, a contributor to The Federalist, and has worked in education policy for the last nine years. https://americanmind.org/memo/get-your-kids-out-of-public-school/.

CHAPTER SIX

The Public School Nightmare That Enslaves the Mind and the Hearts of Your Children.

This is must-read Information for those parents who truly love and care about the souls of their children.

An excellent article on everything you ever suspected about why you and all children should hate the public school system! Keep in mind that the ramifications of this thinking will inevitably lead any parent to attempt to find alternatives: homeschooling, private (very carefully selected) schooling, combinations of the two, and almost any other method. Basically, the public school system is intended to destroy the independent thinking of any and everyone!

The Public-School Nightmare:

Why fix a system designed to destroy individual thought?
by John Taylor Gatto [Two times New York State "Teacher of the Year"]

THE WICKEDNESS OF PUBLIC EDUCATION

I want you to consider the frightening possibility that we are spending far too much money on schooling, not too little. I want you to consider that we have too many people employed in interfering with the way children grow up -- and that all this money and all these people, all the time we take out of children's lives and away from their homes and families and neighborhoods and private explorations -- gets in the way of education.

That seems radical, I know. Surely in modern technological society it is the quantity of schooling and the amount of money you spend on it that buys value.

And yet last year in St. Louis, I heard a vice-president of IBM tell an audience of people assembled to redesign the process of teacher certification that in his opinion this country became computer-literate by self-teaching, not through any action of schools. He said 45 million people were comfortable with computers who had learned through dozens of non-systematic strategies, none of them very formal; if schools had pre-empted the right to teach computer use we would be in a horrible mess right now instead of leading the world in this literacy.

Now think about Sweden, a beautiful, healthy, prosperous and up-to-date country with a spectacular reputation for quality in everything it produces. It makes sense to think their schools must have something to do with that.

Then what do you make of the fact that you can't go to school in Sweden until you are 7 years old? The unsentimental Swedes have wiped out what would be first and second grades because they don't want to pay the large social bill that quickly comes due when boys and girls are ripped away from their best teachers at home too early. It just isn't worth the price, say the Swedes, to provide jobs for teachers and therapists if the result is sick, incomplete kids who can't be put back together again very easily.

The entire Swedish school sequence isn't 12 years, either -- it's nine—less schooling, not more. The direct savings of such a step in the US would be $75-100 billion, a lot less foreclosed home mortgages, a lot of time freed up with which to seek an education.

Who was it that decided to force your attention onto Japan instead of Sweden? Japan with its long school year and state compulsion, instead of Sweden with its short school year, short school sequence, and free choice where your kid is schooled? Who decided you should know about Japan and not Hong Kong, an Asian neighbor with a short school year that outperforms Japan across the board in math and science? Whose interests are served by hiding that from you?

One of the principal reasons we got into the mess we're in is that we allowed schooling to become a very profitable monopoly and guaranteed its customers by the state's police power. Systematic schooling attracts increased investment only when it does poorly, and since there are no penalties at all for such performance, the temptation not to do well is overwhelming.

That's because school staff, both line, and management, are involved in a guild system. And in that ancient form of association, no single member is allowed to outperform any other member; none are allowed to advertise or to introduce new technology or improvise without the advance consent of the guild. Violation of these precepts is severely sanctioned--as Marva Collins, Jaime Escalante and a large number of once-brilliant teachers found out.

The guild reality cannot be broken without returning primary decision-making to parents, letting them buy what they want to buy in schooling, and encouraging the entrepreneurial reality that existed until 1852. That is why I urge any business to think twice before entering a cooperative relationship with the schools we currently have. Cooperating with these places will only make them worse.

The structure of American schooling, 20th-century style, began in 1806 when Napoleon's amateur soldiers beat the professional soldiers of Prussia at the battle of Jena. When your business is selling soldiers, losing a battle like that is serious. Almost immediately afterward a German philosopher named Fichte delivered his famous "Address to the German Nation," which became one of the most influential documents in modern history.

In effect he told the Prussian people that the party was over, that the nation would have to shape up through a new Utopian institution of forced schooling in which everyone would learn to take orders. A dictator actually started the concept of National education. So the world got compulsion schooling at the end of a state bayonet for the first time in human history; modern forced schooling started in Prussia in 1819 with a clear vision of what centralized schools could deliver:

1. Obedient soldiers to the army;
2. Obedient workers to the mines;
3. Well subordinated civil servants to government;
4. Well subordinated clerks to industry
5. Citizens who thought alike about major issues.

Schools should create an artificial national consensus on matters that had been worked out in advance by leading German families and the head of institutions. Schools should create unity among all the German states, eventually unifying them into Greater Prussia. We see this followed through all the way up to Hitler. A whole nation was taken into a demonic and horrible war that engulfed the world.

Prussian industry boomed from the beginning because of brainwashing that made their citizens basically slaves. She was successful in warfare, and her reputation in international affairs was very high. Twenty-six years after this form of schooling began, the King of Prussia was invited to North America to determine the boundary between the United States and Canada. Thirty-three years after that fateful invention of the central school institution, as the behest of Horace Mann and many other leading citizens, we borrowed the style of Prussian schooling as our own.

You need to know this because over the first 50 years, our school's Prussian design -- which was to create a form of state socialism -- gradually forced out our traditional American design, which in most minds was to prepare the individual to be self-reliant.

In Prussia, the purpose of the Volksshule [work school], which educated 92 percent of the children, was not intellectual development but socialization in obedience and subordination. The thinking was left to the Real Schulen, [Real School] in which 8 percent of the kids participated. But for the great mass, intellectual development was regarded with managerial horror as something that caused armies to lose battles.

Prussia concocted a method based on complex fragmentation to ensure that its school products would fit the grand social design. Some of these methods involved dividing whole ideas into school subjects, each further divisible; some of it involved short periods punctuated by a horn so that ceaseless interruptions would mute self-motivation in study.

THE WICKEDNESS OF PUBLIC EDUCATION

There were many more training techniques, but all were built around the premise that isolation from first-hand information, and fragmentation of the abstract information presented by teachers, would result in obedient and subordinate graduates, properly respectful of arbitrary orders.

"Lesser" men would be unable to interfere with policymakers because, while they could still complain, they could not manage sustained or comprehensive thought. Well-schooled children cannot think critically, cannot argue effectively.

One of the most interesting by-products of Prussian schooling turned out to be the two most devastating wars of modern history, World War I and World War II.

Erich Maria Ramarque, in his classic "All Quiet on the Western Front" tells us that the tricks of schoolmasters caused the First World War. The famous Protestant theologian Dietrich Bonhoeffer said that the Second World War was the inevitable product of good schooling.

It's important to underline that Bonhoeffer meant that literally, not metaphorically -- schooling after the Prussian fashion removes the ability of the mind to think for itself. It teaches people to wait for a teacher to tell them what to do and if they have done good or bad. Thus, Prussian teaching paralyzes the moral will as well as the intellect. It's true that sometimes well-schooled students sound smart because they memorize many opinions of great thinkers, but they actually are badly damaged because their own ability to think is left rudimentary and undeveloped.

We got from the United States to Prussia and back because a small number of very passionate ideological leaders visited Prussia in the first half of the 19th century, and fell in love with the order, obedience and efficiency of its system and relentlessly proselytized for a translation of Prussian vision onto these shores.

If Prussia's ultimate goal was the unification of Germany, our major goal, so these men thought, was the unification of hordes of immigrant Catholics into a national consensus based on a northern European cultural model. Of course, to do that, children would have to be removed from their parents and inappropriate cultural influence.

In this fashion, compulsory schooling, a bad idea that had been around at least since Plato's Republic, a bad idea that New England had tried to enforce in 1650 without any success, was finally rammed through the Massachusetts legislature in 1852.

It was, of course, the famous **"Know-Nothing"** legislature that passed this law, a legislature that was the leading edge of a famous secret society which flourished at that time known as **"The Order of the Star Spangled Banner,"** whose password was the simple sentence, **"I know nothing"** -- hence the popular label attached to the secret society's political arm, **"The American Party."**

Over the next 50 years, state after state followed suit, ending schools of choice and surrendering the field to a new government monopoly. There was one powerful exception to this -- the children who could afford to be privately educated. [Although it may be relevant that not ALL private schools are geared to a "real" education, but are simply more of the same as the public schools but are promoted as being for the elite.]

It's important to note that the underlying premise of Prussian schooling is that the government is the true parent of children -- the

THE WICKEDNESS OF PUBLIC EDUCATION

State is sovereign over the family. At the most extreme pole of this notion is the idea that biological parents are really the enemies of their own children, not to be trusted.

How did a Prussian system of dumbing children down take hold in American schools.

Thousands and thousands of young men from prominent American families journeyed to Prussia and other parts of Germany during the 19th century and brought home the Ph. D. degree to a nation in which such a credential was unknown.   These men pre-empted the top positions in the academic world, incorporate research, and in government, to the point where opportunity was almost closed to those who had not studied in Germany, or who were not the direct disciples of a German PhD, as John Dewey was the disciple of G. Stanley Hall at Johns Hopkins.

Virtually every single one of the founders of American schooling had made the pilgrimage to Germany, and many of these men wrote widely circulated reports praising the Teutonic methods. Horace Mann's famous 7th Report of 1844, still available in large libraries, was perhaps the most important of these.

By 1889, a little more than 100 years ago, the crop was ready for harvest. It that year the US Commissioner of Education, William Torrey Harris, assured a railroad magnate, Collis Huntington, that American schools were "scientifically designed" to prevent "over-education" from happening.   The average American would be content with his humble role in life, said the commissioner, because he would not be tempted to think about any other role. My guess is that Harris meant he would not be able to think about any other role.

In 1896 the famous John Dewey, then at the University of Chicago, said that independent, self-reliant people were a counter-productive anachronism in the collective society of the future. In modern society, said Dewey, people would be defined by their associations --not by their own individual accomplishments. In such a world, people who read too well or too early are dangerous because they become privately empowered, they know too much, and know how to find out what they don't know by themselves, without consulting experts.

Dewey said the great mistake of traditional pedagogy was to make reading and writing constitute the bulk of early schoolwork. He advocated the phonics method of teaching reading be abandoned and replaced by the whole word method, not because the latter was more efficient (he admitted that it was less efficient), but because independent thinkers were produced by hard books, thinkers who cannot be socialized very easily.

By socialization Dewey meant a program of social objectives administered by the best social thinkers in government. This was a giant step on the road to state socialism. The method of indoctrination was pioneered in Prussia. It is a vision radically disconnected with the American past, its historic hopes and dreams.

Dewey's former professor and close friend, G. Stanley Hall, said this at about the same time, "Reading should no longer be a fetish. Little attention should be paid to reading."

Hall was one of the three men most responsible for building a gigantic administrative infrastructure over the classroom. How enormous that structure became can only be understood by comparisons: New York State, for instance, employs more school administrators than all of the European Economic Community nations combined.

Once you truly understand that the control of conduct is what schools are about, the word "reform" takes on a very particular meaning. It means making adjustments to the machine so that young subjects will not twist and turn so, while their minds and bodies are being scientifically controlled. Helping kids to use their minds better is it is completely contrary to the public school's vision.

Bertrand Russell once said that American schooling was among the most radical experiments in human history, that America was deliberately denying its children the tools of critical thinking.

When you want to teach children to think, you begin by treating them seriously when they are little, giving them responsibilities, talking to them candidly, providing privacy and solitude for them, and making them readers and thinkers of significant thoughts from the beginning. That's if you want to teach them to think. There is no evidence that this has been the purpose since the start of compulsory schooling.

When Frederich Froebel, the inventor of kindergarten in 19th century Germany, fashioned his idea he did not have a "garden for children" in mind, but a metaphor of teachers as gardeners and children as the vegetables.

Kindergarten was created to be a way to break the influence of parents on their children. I note with interest the growth of daycare in the US and the repeated urgings to extend school downward to include 4-year-olds. The movement toward state socialism is not some historical curiosity but a powerful dynamic force in the world around us.

The state socialism movement is fighting for its life against those forces which would, through vouchers or tax credits, deprive it of financial lifeblood, and it has countered this thrust with a demand for even more control over children's lives, and even more money to pay for the extended school day and year that this control requires. A movement as visibly destructive to individuality, family and community as government-system schooling has been, might be expected to collapse in the face of its dismal record, coupled with an increasingly aggressive shakedown of the taxpayer, but this has not happened.

The explanation is largely found in the transformation of schooling from a simple service to families and towns to an enormous, centralized corporate enterprise. While this development has had a markedly adverse effect on people and on our democratic traditions, it has made schooling the single largest employer in the United States and the largest grantor of contracts next to the Defense Department.

Both of these low-visibility phenomena provide monopoly schooling with powerful political friends, publicists, advocates and other useful allies. This is a large part of the explanation why no amount of failure ever changes things in schools or changes them for very long. School people are able to outlast any storm and to keep short attention-span public scrutiny thoroughly confused.

An overview of the short history of this institution reveals a pattern marked by intervals of public outrage, followed by enlargement of the monopoly in every case. After nearly 30 years spent inside a number of public schools, some considered good, some bad, I feel certain that management cannot clean its own house. On the contrary, it relentlessly marginalizes all significant change.

THE WICKEDNESS OF PUBLIC EDUCATION

There are no incentives for the "owners" of the structure to reform it, nor can there be without outside competition. What is needed for several decades is the kind of wildly-swinging free market we had at the beginning of our national history.

It cannot be overemphasized that no body of theory exists to accurately define the way children learn, or which learning is of most worth. By pretending the existence of such we have cut ourselves off from the information and innovation that only a real free market can provide. Fortunately, our national situation has been so favorable, so dominant through most of our history, that the margin of error afforded has been vast.

But the future is not so clear. Violence, narcotic addictions, divorce, alcoholism, loneliness... all these are but tangible measures of abject poverty in America's educational system. Surely schools, as the institutions monopolizing the daytimes of childhood, can be called to account for this. In a Republic, the final judges cannot be experts, but only the people.

Trust the people, give them choices, and the school nightmare will vanish in a generation.

http://www.halexandria.org/dward036.htm

PUBLIC EDUCATION IS TERRIFYING

The reports coming out of the school systems of Portland, Ore., and its suburbs are simply terrifying. Children are being taught the narrative that America is fundamentally evil, and the rioters who continue to wreak havoc on that once-beautiful, quiet city are held up as heroes. As Christopher Rufo has reported, "The schools have self-consciously adopted the 'pedagogy of the oppressed as their theoretical orientation, activated through a curriculum of critical race theory and enforced through the appointment of de facto political officers within individual schools."

And it is working. The schools have become, Rufo notes, "a school-to-radicalism pipeline."

But it is not just in radicalized Portland or Seattle where these forces hold sway. In my own home county of Loudoun County, Va., the radicals have seized control and plunged with abandon in a radical direction, leaving much of our community gasping at the temerity of their tactics and shuddering at the implications for the future of our community and our nation should they succeed.

It Isn't Just Conservative Parents Opposing Critical Race Theory in Schools

Loudoun is the school district that suspended its teacher, Tanner Cross, for having the audacity to speak for one minute at a recent school board meeting in opposition to a proposed sexual/political mandate. Let that sink in. Before the policy was in place, a highly regarded teacher was suspended for simply disagreeing with a proposed policy.

The legal organization I lead, Alliance Defending Freedom, represents Tanner. I was astounded when, in the midst of a hearing seeking a temporary injunction to reinstate him, which the court granted Tuesday, the school district's lawyer volunteered the fact that he was the eighth employee in the past two years who has been suspended for out-of-school speech. Apparently, consistently violating the First Amendment rights of its employees makes everything all right in the minds of this school district.

THE WICKEDNESS OF PUBLIC EDUCATION

Parents know that the curriculum has recently turned hard to the left. Racial and sexual politics are the prime directive of the school system. Every child will be immersed. And every teacher will recite the party line. No dissenting allowed.

The school district seems oblivious to the fact that they are losing not just conservative parents, but the great bulk of the middle-of-the road families who simply want their children to get a quality academic education.

The leadership of the Loudoun County Public Schools may be woke, but they are blind. They do not seem to see the growing signs of an educational revolution that is stirring in communities across the nation. Parents have simply had enough of the politicization of their local schools and the attempts to turn their children into young but full-throated activists for the progressive movement.

Parents don't want their children taught that they are oppressors if they have the wrong skin color. Teaching little white kids that they are evil because of their race is wicked, just as it was when the worst schools of our past taught little black children that they were intellectually inferior because of their race.

 Vanishingly few parents want their children immersed in a one-sided racial vendetta seeking to blame seven-year-olds for the acts of some people with the same skin color from past generations. This is racial scapegoating, growing from the same depraved ideology that in times past has conferred guilt and blame on entire people groups based solely on race.

IT IS TIME TO ABANDON THE PUBLIC SCHOOL SYSTEM!

Teachers Unions Pushing for Mandatory Masks, Vaccines for Students

Teachers' unions in several states are continuing to push for mandatory masks and vaccines for students while demanding the right to choose for adults.

The Hawaii State Department of Health issued "guidance" for public schools, according to Hawaii News Now, which: Promotes (but does not require) COVID-19 [Chinese coronavirus] vaccines as a "core essential strategy,"

Recommends universal mask-wearing indoors and, when in groups, outdoors.

The agency left open the possibility of mandating a vaccination to participate in extracurricular activities. Hawaii State Teachers Association President Osa Tui Jr. was unhappy with the recommendations.

"There's going to be a lot of interactions where you're on top of others and things like that. Maybe mandating for those types of extracurricular activities is the right step," he said.

Tui opposed a vaccine mandate for teachers and staff, claiming "it won't work." "It doesn't make sense to have a school with all personnel vaccinated but not your students. So, if you're going to mandate the personnel to get vaccinated, the students should get vaccinated," he said.

THE WICKEDNESS OF PUBLIC EDUCATION

Meanwhile, the Mississippi Association of Educators are pressuring state bureaucrats to issue mandates after Gov. Tate Reeves (R) declined. The union has a beef with the Mississippi Department of Health's recommendation that only unvaccinated residents be masked, writing in an open letter reported by Mississippi Today:

"It is imperative that schools see state-led intervention beyond advising mask wear among unvaccinated students and educators. This policy has the potential to create more problems than it solves: How will we determine who is and is not vaccinated? Are there repercussions for lying about vaccination status or choosing not to wear a mask if you are unvaccinated? Who is responsible for confirming a student's vaccination status?" the letter said. "Simply put: It is unfair to ask educators to become their school's vaccination police when putting on a mask will help keep the entire school community safe and healthy."

The teacher's union helped write a policy for Illinois's Springfield School District 186 that would require "pre-kindergarten, elementary and middle school students who cannot receive COVID-19 vaccinations to wear face masks indoors throughout the school day," according to the State Journal-Register.

Board member Micah Miller "said he would support a policy that required masks for those students who are unvaccinated or unwilling to share their vaccination status," the paper reported.

"I'm happy to see us relying on the experts of medicine in our community and in our state, as well as working in conjunction with the SEA (Springfield teachers union)," board member Buffy Lael-Wolf said.

Newsweek reported in May that the American Federation of Teachers, the country's second-largest school employees union, "will continue to push for face masks to be worn in schools," regardless of vaccination status or what the Centers for Disease Control and Prevention (CDC) recommends.

CHAPTER SEVEN

A Godless Heathen Public School System!

There is nothing more damning and destructive to America's youth today than the Godless public school system!

I thank God for the Bill of Rights. I thank God for the wisdom of our founding fathers. I thank God for the First Amendment, which gives us the legal right to freedom of speech, press, religion, and the right to peaceably assemble and protest. I am exercising my God-given freedom, by publishing this desperately needed article about the Godless and heathen public school system. There is no evil today as wicked as the Communist, humanistic, sexually immoral public school system. I detest the public school system! It is destructive to the faith of children!

Sex Education Program in Our Public Schools: What Is Behind It?

Perhaps you are asking, "What is so wrong with the public school system? In a word, EVERYTHING! Perhaps a better question is: What is right about the public school system? The truth is intolerant my friend. $1 + 1 = 2$. Now you can ignorantly claim that $1 + 1 = 3$; but you'd be wrong (and probably a product of the public school system).

*Here is a comment I just received on Facebook about this very thing.

Jennifer Humphrey
Last year we were virtual learners in the district. I was floored the first time I heard the teacher do this. She would ask what does 2+2 equal. And a child would say 5. The teacher could not tell them they were wrong. She would say something like, I like your answer, you worked really hard to figure that out, now let's try to solve it this way.

Children are being robbed of their faith in God in public schools. Instead, children are taught that they evolved from "stardust" which somehow formed into a planet, and then life just happened. Children are taught that humans are animals. If this is true, then bestiality is acceptable, right? This is what the evolutionists teach, is it not?

Satan's crowd fully understands that children are a weapon in the hands of the Devil, which the Holy Bible confirms. Psalms 127:4, "As arrows are in the hand of a mighty man; so are children of the youth." He who controls today's youth, sets the future. The communist dictator Vladimir Lenin also understood this truth, who said: "The best revolutionary is a youth devoid of morals."

If you grasp this truth, it becomes obvious why wicked men have usurped control of the government's public education system! Satan wants to kill, steal, and destroy your children and your family! It is not a coincidence that children's public school curriculum is so senseless and confusing that parents cannot even help their children do their homework. They are intentionally dumbing down the children!

THE WICKEDNESS OF PUBLIC EDUCATION

A good Christian family is a bulwark for good morals, the soil for planting good character, the tool and means for furthering Biblical Christianity and confirming it upon the earth. The family is also the foundation of the nation, as Philaret, Metropolitan of Moscow, wrote, "In the family lie the seeds of everything that later sprouts and grows into the greater family which is called the nation." Satan knows this truth better than any Christian. Why do you think the family is under demonic attack from all sides?

The Bible, God's Word, foretold that the time would come when people would be lovers of their own selves, woefully ignorant of the truth. We are certainly living in such a time. The same sun that melts the wax hardens the clay. I'd like to quote some Scriptures from the Word of God (i.e., the King James Bible)...

2 Timothy 3: 1 This know also, that in the last days perilous times shall come.2 For men shall be lovers of their own selves, covetous, boasters, proud, blasphemers, disobedient to parents, unthankful, unholy,3 Without natural affection, trucebreakers, false accusers, incontinent, fierce, despisers of those that are good,4 Traitors, heady, highminded, lovers of pleasures more than lovers of God;5 Having a form of godliness, but denying the power thereof: from such turn away.

Faith MUST come before secular knowledge. Character must come before natural knowledge. To educate a man beyond his character is to produce an educated fool **(Romans 1:22, "Professing themselves to be wise, they became fools").** To educate a man who lacks faith in God is to produce a generation of wicked men.

Psalm 10:4The wicked, through the pride of his countenance, will not seek after God: God is not in all his thoughts.

The public school system produces educated fools. Young children who should be taught about God are instead brainwashed with Evolution and worldly philosophies. I call Evolution, Devilution, and for good reason (Hitler was a big fan of Charles Darwin's The Origin of Species). Communism, Nazism, Godlessness, and Evolution are all synonymous in ideologies. Welcome to the public school detention camp. America's schoolchildren long ago were taught HOW TO THINK, but for the past half-century have been taught WHAT TO THINK!

"Education is a weapon, whose effect depends on who holds it in his hands and at whom it is aimed." —Communist dictator, Joseph Stalin (1934)

http://www.jesus-is-savior.com/Family/public_schools_are_evil.htm

Am I a Girl or a Boy?

Even if the parents are excellent parents and discipline their children at home, the public teaching system destroys their training at home.

I have had to deal with two families as their pastors where the education system convinced their boys that they were not boys. They convinced them that they were girls. They did not let these young men make that decision, they corrupted their minds with their twisted ungodly philosophies. Sincerely Dr. Michael H Yeager

DID YOU KNOW

Liberal Teachers Are the Predominant Teachers in the Public School System!

There are 79 Democrats in the teaching profession for every 21 Republicans.

At the High School level, there are 87 Democrats for every 13 Republicans.

In elementary schools, there are 85 Democrats for every 15 Republicans.

As an adolescent, just beginning my education as a Catholic, I had Catechism classes. These classes were usually an hour lawn, where we learned some of the basic tenets of the Roman Catholic faith. In other denominations, this is known as Sunday School. I suppose the true purpose of Sunday School is edification and the equipping of the pupils with a solid foundation in religious faith. Progressive Liberals have their own Sunday School. Of course, given that they tout a Trojan Horse religion, they get away with not calling it what it is. It is a total indoctrination into their wicked and ungodly beliefs.

As a teacher and a former public-school student, I have become intimately acquainted with the inner workings of the Progressive Liberal Sunday School catechizing the youth of America. Over 50 million young people attend public schools every year. About 56.4 million students are projected to attend elementary, middle, and high schools across the United States. Of the 50.7 million public school students: 1.5 million are expected to attend prekindergarten.

3.7 million are expected to attend kindergarten.

To an overwhelming extent, public schools indoctrinate their minds to accept and think uncritically about basic Progressive Liberal doctrines by the priests and priestesses who teach their classes.

Within the schools that teach the teachers, Social Sciences—which the university Schools of Education fall under—registered Democrats outnumber Republican Professors by a margin of over 10 to 1. Even in my Jesuit School of Education, we were heavy on social justice but weak on the classical canon of literature; we went deep into the all-powerful influence of racism, sexism, class, and other bigoted isms as applied to education, but we hardly ever talked about the Western tradition of liberty, the pursuit of truth, and the search for the meaning of life.

It should come as no surprise that K-12 teachers in America adhere overwhelmingly to the Progressive Liberal faith. Verdant Labs, using Federal Election Commission data showing the professions of those who contribute to political campaigns, created some educated guesses about how Republican or Democratic certain professions are. The data on my profession, teaching, was unsurprising.

PS: Shockingly, we as Christians are turning our children over to be educated by God-haters!

https://www.amgreatness.com/2019/06/11/k-12-education-has-become-progressive-sunday-school/

Public Education Will Take Your Children to Hell

THE WICKEDNESS OF PUBLIC EDUCATION

One of the most destructive forces in the lives of children today is state-run public schools. Their children are subject to torture and abuse at the hands of other children. So let me ask you a question. If you get beaten up by somebody else at School and they happened to be 11 years old, does that change the trauma you experienced?

What if a 30-year-old beat up an 11-year-old? What would we do? We put them in jail because it's a crime, and yet it happens all the time in public School to these little children. Have you heard about the 11-year-old boy in Georgia who jumped out of a school bus to escape bullying?

This is from the New York post by someone named Tamara lapping. This article appears on May 20th, 2021. It begins with an 11-year-old boy jumped out of a school bus to escape beating by bullies. Then, he jumped onto a passing pickup truck in a desperate attempt to escape his bullies.

His father: Dion Murphy, told Fox five in Atlanta that his son fled out of a bus window. Last Wednesday, as other students were beating him, one student jumped in his face. He was pushing him against the window. When he fell, the other student took his shoe, and in a desperate attempt to escape these bullies, he jumped out the window. Murphy said the bus was stopped at a turn lane.

When the middle-schooler leaped out of the right rear window, he landed on a passing pickup truck before rolling onto the highway. The Georgia state patrol said the child, a student at the youth middle school in Walton county was taken to a local hospital. He suffered a concussion and a broken elbow. What kind of trauma do you think this is going to cause this boy for the rest of his life?

Now it was not the first-time bullies had picked on him. The family said they had alerted the school about previous incidents in which the School had done nothing. This time it was so bad that the boy was trying to escape before he was seriously hurt.

Murphy said he had seen a video of them beating his son that they showed him during a meeting with the School's principal on Friday. As a parent myself, I am so upset because the school neglect to stop these bullies. It did not do anything about it. So let me ask you a question. Who's to blame for what happened? Is it the school? You might say Oh, yes, it is the school. They should have done something before this ever happened. And I agree they should do something about what was happening to this young boy. They should have done something about all these kids that were involved.

But let us be honest about this situation. It is the father of this boy who is to blame. He put his son into an environment where he could be abused. Then, when the abuse started, he let it continue without getting seriously involved. The father said this is not the first time this happened. How many times did this happen until his son tried to escape for his life?

I was telling my wife about this. She said: in our neighborhood there was someone who said that their son, a middle-schooler, was punched in the face on the bus. How many more children must get beat up before you realize that these institutions are evil. They are not in your best interest. They are not in your children's best interest.

In addition to physical and verbal abuse, kids our being taught godless ideas and philosophies. Five days a week, nine months out of the year, their minds and hearts are filled with garbage.

THE WICKEDNESS OF PUBLIC EDUCATION

Christian parents wonder why their children are walking away from God at 12 or 13 years of age. I've said it before, and I will say it again: here is why you lose them. Listen to me. Now you might think, well, who is this guy telling me what to do? It would be best if you listened to me because somebody needs to tell you the truth. The Bible says, do not be deceived evil company, corrupts, good habits. And the Bible says that he walks with the fools will be destroyed.

Here's what happens. You're taking your children to church with you. And that is wonderful if you can get them to go to church with you. By the way, if you say go, they need to go because you're in charge and not them. You teach them to do what is right. You love them with the love of God. You pray for them with deep concern. Remember you only get them two or three hours a day, and the world gets them eight or 10 hours a day.

Many times, even when they are home they're on their phone chatting with their friends and looking up YouTube videos. The world has got them by the throat day in and day out and day out and day in. You are not going to overcome all of this corruption in three hours a night.

What the world does in 10 hours a day, and over the course of years, is extremely destructive. Your child cannot help but begin to think like the world, believe like the world, act like the world, and eventually deny God's existence. Why you say? Because that's what they were trained to do.

It is a massive miracle if you end up with a genuinely godly child who comes out of this wicked and ungodly public education system. Why? Because God said, if you put them in that environment all the time, they're going to end up just like that environment.

Imagine a faithful family, in Israel, in ancient times. Imagine these little Jewish boys and girls, and they're faithful to your way. They go to the temple. They give tithes. They give alms and follow the Jewish customs. They get up every morning and they're happy.

They make breakfast, and they pat little Johnny on the head. The parents walk their children down the street and they are so happy. Then they stop in front of this big, impressive building, and they say, two little Johnny and Susie, here you go. They hand them over to a man or a woman who are complete strangers to the family. They take them into this large building. As you back away from the scene and you see the sign up on the building that they walk into, it says the temple of Moloch. This is the public education system.

THE WORSHIP OF MOLECH!

Moloch also spelled Molech, a Canaanite deity associated in biblical sources with the practice of child sacrifice. The name derives from combining the consonants of the Hebrew melech ("king") with the vowels of boshet ("shame"), the latter often being used in the Old Testament as a variant name for the popular God Baal ("Lord").

In the Hebrew Bible, Moloch is presented as a foreign deity who was at times illegitimately given a place in Israel's worship as a result of the policies of certain apostate kings. The laws given to Moses by God expressly forbade the Jews to do what was done in Egypt or in Canaan. "You shall not give any of your children to devote them by fire to Moloch, and so profane the name of your God" (Leviticus 18:21).

Yet kings such as Ahaz (2 Kings 16:3) and Manasseh (2 Kings 21:6), having been influenced by the Assyrians, are reported to have worshipped Moloch at the Mountain site of Topheth, outside the walls of Jerusalem. This site flourished under Manasseh's son King Amon but was destroyed during the reign of Josiah, the reformer. "And he defiled Topheth, which is in the valley of the sons of Hinnom, that no one might burn his son or his daughter as an offering to Moloch" (2 Kings 23:10).

There are many scriptures that forbid giving your children over to the wicked, and to false gods. The God of communism, liberalism, sexual perversion, humanism and evolutionism. Yet **85%** of the Christians in America turn their children over to these false gods nine months out of the year.

Psalm 106:36 And they served their idols: which were a snare unto them.37 Yea, they sacrificed their sons and their daughters unto devils,38 And shed innocent blood, even the blood of their sons and of their daughters, whom they sacrificed unto the idols of Canaan: and the land was polluted with blood.

Ezekiel 16:20 Moreover thou hast taken thy sons and thy daughters, whom thou hast borne unto me, and these hast thou sacrificed unto them to be devoured. Is this of thy whoredoms a small matter,21 That thou hast slain my children, and delivered them to cause them to pass through the fire for them?

---

2 Kings 17:16 And they left all the commandments of the Lord their God, and made them molten images, even two calves, and

made a grove, and worshipped all the host of heaven, and served Baal.17 And they caused their sons and their daughters to pass through the fire, and used divination and enchantments, and sold themselves to do evil in the sight of the Lord, to provoke him to anger.

Now imagine what God is thinking of this situation. Imagine what kind of adults that your children are going to turn out to be. We as a nation are now seeing the devastating consequences of this evil institution. Look around you, my friends, and ask yourself how many more of our children are we going to condemn to an eternal and godless damnation? How many more grandchildren do you have to lose before you see that we are the ones who have been sacrificing them to devils through the educational system of this world?

How many more do we have to lose before we wake up? There are other options. God has provided both Christian schools and home schools as alternatives to the education of our children.

As parents, we have homeschooled for over 20 years. You might say that we cannot afford it. Ask yourself: what is the worth and the value of your children's souls?

I say unto you that we cannot afford not to raise them in the ways of God. Jesus said: what does it profit a man if he gains the whole world loses his own soul. Fathers and mothers, what does it profit? Many of you go to the beach two weeks a year, and you have three cars. You have all the gadgets, because you have a nice career, but what good is it if you lose your children to the devil.

Millions of so-called Christians have done it and are doing it year after year, decade after decade. Mom says I am unable to homeschool. Yes, you can. God would never command something that he would not provide the grace to do. I use my wife as an example. She does not have a college degree. She did not even like going to school. She did not like educational classes. She does not consider herself to be an intellectual, but she trained all of our children for 20 years at home.

Why? Because she was not going to lose them to the world. Many times she cried at night, as she struggled with giving the children the proper education. Many times, we barely had the money to buy the homeschool books because I had to pay the taxes to cover the pagan schools and I still had to pay for the education for our children.

There are options. You can change friends. You don't have to keep going the way the world is going. You don't have to lose your little ones to the world, the flesh, and the devil. But, for their eternal soul's sake, pay the price to save their souls.

OUR CHILDREN'S MINDS ARE BEING CORRUPTED!

It isn't just a matter of actively teaching that America and the West are evil. Suppression of "wrongthink" is equally as important to the brainwashing process.The young adults who today gleefully tear down statues of the Founding Fathers were incubated in our very own schools.

Conservatives must demand an end to the indoctrination of our youth or face a new American public taught since childhood that the country shouldn't exist. Your children are being indoctrinated. The education system designed to teach them how to think critically has been weaponized by the radical left to push an anti-

American agenda.

As someone who has worked in education for four years, I have seen firsthand how the left and their teachers are ensnaring your children.

I worked with kids from ages 3 to 13 and saw the brainwashing that exists at all levels of education. The left uses a combination of propaganda and suppression to push kids into the ensnaring grip of socialism and anti-patriotism.

First is the propaganda. Teachers will assign work instilling the idea that the pillars of Western civilization were evil, and their memories deserve to be thrown in the trash.

Here's an example. I was helping one of my elementary school students with a homework assignment about listing famous Britons throughout history. Of course, she already had some of the more obvious ones: Shakespeare, Princess Diana, Queen Elizabeth.

"Well, how about Winston Churchill?" I recommended.

"Oh no, not him," she replied. "He was a racist and didn't think women should have rights. He wasn't a good guy."

I was floored. It clearly wasn't something she came up with on her own. She was just regurgitating propaganda her teacher had taught her. All sense of nuance and critical thinking about the man who saved Europe from the Nazis was gone. Churchill committed "wrongthink," so in the bin he goes.

Another way the left propagandizes is through the normalization of its views and positions as nonpolitical.

THE WICKEDNESS OF PUBLIC EDUCATION

The Black Lives Matter organization is a prime example of this. Many of my colleagues wore Black Lives Matter pins and apparel to school in blatant violation of school rules forbidding political statements on clothing.

When I asked for a justification of the behavior, I was told it wasn't political to support the group, it was a matter of human rights. The children would see these pins and clothes and connect radical leftist groups with basic human dignity. "How dare you question Black Lives Matter? I was taught this is a matter of human rights!"

But it isn't just a matter of actively teaching that America and the West are evil. Suppression of "wrong think" is equally as important to the brainwashing process. The lessons I was allowed to teach also were censored.

I was preparing a lesson on Thanksgiving involving Pilgrims and American Indians, with an activity centered on making paper teepees for arts and crafts. Cue the progressive panic.

Other teachers at the school were incensed that a non-Indian was "appropriating" Native American culture for an activity. Of course, these teachers weren't Indians either, they just wanted to virtue signal.

The whole thing culminated in a hilarious incident where my colleagues tracked down the one teacher on staff who was one-sixty-fourths Native American and asked her if it was cultural appropriation. In her esteemed authority, it most certainly was. The school administrators pulled me aside and promptly nixed the project.

The suppression extends to American religious values as well. I would try to engage my students with folk stories from around the globe to teach them world history and other cultures.

Storytime went on without a hitch until I decided to tell stories from the Bible. Other teachers began to complain I was preaching Christian values to the children and attempting to convert them.

Keep in mind, this wasn't a problem when I was sharing stories from other ancient cultures throughout history. Stories about ancient India and China were fine and encouraged as "sharing unheard voices." After sharing the story of the Tower of Babel, I was told to switch back to non-Christian stories or face the consequences.

The young adults who today gleefully tear down statues of the Founding Fathers were incubated in our very own schools, groomed to burst from the education system and burn America down.

The left argues the great men and women who built this nation are problematic and must be destroyed. Conservatives must demand an end to the indoctrination of our youth or face a new American public taught since childhood that the country shouldn't exist.

This piece originally appeared in The Daily Signal.

.

CHAPTER EIGHT

The "Evils" of Public Schools

This article was initially printed in educational Horizons Fall 2001 by Edward G. Rozycki, Ed. D.

He who passively accepts evil is as much involved in it as he who helps to perpetuate it. He who accepts evil without protesting against it is really cooperating with it.
--- Martin Luther King

Introduction

My fifth-grade experience in Longfellow public school was a joy, a really educational experience.1 Sixth grade was another story. My sixth-grade teacher, Mrs. P. was much taken by my "artistic ability. "One fine day, she told me, "You're going to enter the Gimbel's Department Store Art Contest on Healthy Living and win a prize!" I was somewhat flattered and excited at the thought that I would be permitted to while away several weeks of afternoons painting at a poster rather than following along the prescribed curriculum.

I began planning a poster on Healthy Living. What might I do? "Never you mind about that, "said Mrs. P.,"I have an old poster here you can just copy! Look! Isn't it wonderful?"

I was speechless. I was being told to do something that -- even then -- I recognized as deep-down dishonest. But the importunity was not coming, as it usually did, from classmates who were already seeing to my loss of innocence by teaching me -- with full details -- an obscenity a day. No, the temptation was coming from a member of that moral aristocracy, Teachers, who - my parents had drilled into me - were **Ones Who Must Be Obeyed, Ones Who Knew Best What Was Good For Me.**

I summoned up the courage to say that I didn't want to copy someone else's work. Mrs. P. responded,"I'm very disappointed in you. It's either paint this poster or do arithmetic drills." So I painted.

With disgust and loathing, I finished the poster. It was better than the original. Every one admired it, especially She Who Had to Be Obeyed, Who Knew Best What Was Good For Me. The poster was hung up in the front of the room for general approbation while awaiting shipment to the exhibition.

I don't know what came over me. A day after finishing it, right after lunch, I walked up to that vile poster and took a dish of black paint, and spattered it onto the painting. I trembled, confused with the righteousness of my disobedience.

I hurried back outside, believing no one had seen me. I was wrong.

THE WICKEDNESS OF PUBLIC EDUCATION

Carolyn N. was a witness and ran to tattle to Mrs. P who berated me as soon as I returned to class. She put me on a diet of four-place addition drills with no recess for two weeks. Strangely, she didn't call my parents and inform them of my "misbehavior." Dear sweet Carolyn, at Mrs. P's behest, cleaned up the poster. It was submitted in my name. It won a prize. When my parents and Mrs. P. accompanied me to the awards ceremonies, they remarked about how indifferent I seemed to the honor.

Such incidents are not restricted to public schools. I know, for example, of two private schools -- one, of the ancient elite -- where the headmasters sold drugs to the students. Only one headmaster was caught. But, in general, private education takes a quite different view of wrongdoing than the view that is promulgated in public schools. Private education, thus, is, by its own definitions, not susceptible to the faults attributable to public education.

Even though parochial school kids no longer come home bearing tales of nuns wielding yardsticks in the classroom like Crusaders slaying heathen, I have gotten recent complaints by students in those schools that extended periods of class time before public elections were used to write letters to support political agendas. Students were told to sign their parents' names without asking permission even though the parents of the students might well have opposed or taken no position on the political issue. Corruption of educational mission is not unique to public education.

Public schools do provide opportunities for corruption for five interrelated reasons:

a. they are schools of last resort in a compulsory system;

b. this makes them susceptible to constraint by underinformed courts to institute procedures often contrary to good educational practice;

c. special, often ephemeral, interest groups can gain control over school practices by combining vociferousness with legal ingenuity;

d. not only naive idealists but the weak-minded and pathologically sentimental are seduced into assuming teaching positions which they -- often with good reason -- abandon at the national rate of 13% per year; consequently

e. surviving educators do not possess a sufficient sense of profession to take risks opposing those whose efforts, in the long run, distort and demean the educational mission -- for which no practicable consensus exists -- of the public school.

EXAMPLE OF INSANITY OF A BOY NAMED PETER!

My recent re-viewing provoked my memories of my sixth-grade artistic award -- perhaps the tenth -- of the video called: Educating Peter in a class of graduate students in education. (I watch this video about twice a year.) "You can watch this video for free on YouTube". The plot: An under socialized, physically abusive White male child who has Down's syndrome is placed into a third-grade class with an teacher whose sole preparation seems to be in rationalizing why onions are like peaches, if only you taste them the right way.

The teacher, unable to handle Peter even with the help of what appears to be an extra adult, compels her students -- with the complicity of school staff -- to "take ownership of the situation." A few sessions of psychobabble indoctrination bring the third graders to comprehend the causal complexities of Peter's behavior and their role in provoking it. This means that now it is expected that

THE WICKEDNESS OF PUBLIC EDUCATION

Peter's behavioral outbursts -- even the violent ones -- will be interdicted by the students rather than by the teacher.

The teacher -- in an interview -- tells how it is important, in this all-White school in Virginia, that her students learn to live with people different than themselves. She tells how by "raising her expectations" -- one imagines her commanding her synapses to fire in unison, her dendrites to do drills -- Peter is brought to make academic progress.

We see students reacting with shock and dismay to Peter's behavior. The adults in the video (and the narrator) assure us that these students are "learning to accept differences." There is no evidence for this remote probability. From the looks of things, they could just as well be learning resignation in the face of power, both Peter's power and that of the adults who condone what to them as "normal kids" is forbidden.

The students, choked, kicked, pushed by Peter are encouraged to rationalize, to declare that Peter has become their best friend. Peter has taught them more than he himself has learned, that this has been just the peachy-keenest of classes. The students blush as they are interviewed, not being able -- unlike the adults who provide them example -- to suppress the natural embarrassment the innocent feel about deliberately mouthing what they believe to be false.

The film purports to be not taking sides in the controversy about inclusion but merely "telling a story." It is cleverly edited to produce a certain effect. I remember an earlier version which I had seen some years ago. It was different from the version I purchased from Ambrose Video Publishing. A crucial scene has been edited out.

In the early version, the boys are sitting outside in a field. Peter, unprovoked, kicks a boy square in the middle of the face. Here the cut occurs. The other boy, outraged, jumps on Peter. The teacher intervened and reprimanded the boy who was kicked. They show this boy crying by himself, uncounseled by an adult.

In the present version, one sees the kick and then the boy crying, alone and uncounseled. That he should not be consoled is inexplicable, assuming there are adults present. But knowing he has just been rebuked -- which has been spliced out of the film -- explains the lack of consolation. The boy's isolation is part of his "punishment" for "fighting" back.

At the end of the year, we find Peter "accepted" into the group, having -- in the words of his teacher -- "fewer outbursts, mostly toward the end of the day."

One of my students remarked that what the third graders had accomplished was akin to changing a dangerous animal into a pet. Peter was exempted from normal discipline, clearly treated to be of diminished responsibility, and given almost bizarrely effusive encouragement and reward for trivial accomplishments. He was "managed."

The students who watched Educating Peter with me were asked to pay attention to four questions: What are the benefits of including Peter in the third-grade classroom? What is the benefit? What are the costs of including Peter in the third-grade classroom? Who pays the cost of his involvement?

Peter's education could be seen as a form of charity bestowed on the less fortunate. But it is a debauched form of "charity" that comes through a compulsory system. Our courts have decided that the practice of inclusion is an improvement on justice. But the lopsided redistribution of scarce schooling resources -- where the needs of some take precedence over the needs of many -- may just bring about every child's educational starvation.

Top Five Reasons NOT to Send Your Kids Back to Public School

By Pastor Voddie Baucham

Anyone who has kept up with my blog knows that I am no fan of government education. I have made it a point to carry The Continuing Collapse on a regular basis, and I try to make biblical, philosophical, and theological arguments in favor of Christian education as often as possible. However, I recognize the obstacles those of us on my side of the street face. As many as eighty-five to ninety percent of professing Christians send their children to the government for their education.

That is simply an astonishing figure since the Christian community fought mandatory government education tooth-and-nail for its first fifty years of existence. Since then, we have gone from fighting against government schools to fighting for them and implying that those who fight against them are fundamentalists, anti-intellectuals, and racists.

In the meantime, our schools grow progressively worse. As fall approaches, I want to appeal to those of you with children in government schools. Please don't send them back! I beg you to consider what you are doing. As Dave Black has written: "No academic skepticism, no secularist authors, no blatant materialism can so undermine the spiritual life of the country like the completely secularized training of the child under the authority of the state. Bible-based education is mandatory for Christian parents. If we think we can keep our children in a secular school system and escape the dumbed-down, amoral, and immoral results of secular humanism in schools, we are sorely mistaken.

With that, here are the top five reasons not to send your kids back to government/public school.

5. You Don't Have To

This may sound like a no-brainer, but you'd be surprised how many people ask home educators the 'authority' questions (i.e., to whom do you report? Who approves your curriculum?). These questions are the byproduct of statism. The Gramscian, neo-Marxist influence is so prevalent in our culture that we don't even recognize it anymore. We believe that children are wards of the state when in fact they are not.

 As a result, some people have a hard time believing that they have the right to educate their children in a manner of their choosing. Well, I'm here to tell you that you are free. Your children are yours. They do not belong to Caesar. You don't have to take them back to the local government indoctrination center next semester. And in some states (thank God for Texas), you don't even have to tell them you're not coming back!

4. America's Schools Are Among the Worst in the Industrialized World

One of the issues that many Christians seem willing to ignore is the fact that sending children to American schools represents extremely poor stewardship. American students continually rank at the bottom in math, science, and reading compared to other industrialized nations. That's right; our educational system is among the world's worst! Of course, everyone says, "Our schools are different." News flash… that's a lie!

One of our elders taught honors math at one of the 'best schools in one of the 'best school districts in Texas (you know, one of those school's people lie and cheat to get their children into so that they can get a 'better education). Unfortunately, his advanced geometry class was filled with a bunch of imbeciles who could barely do basic arithmetic. As a result, most of them failed their first major test. You know what happened next?

The principal called him into the office and told him to make things right. One of the things he was told was to employ a grading technique called "Square root times ten." Thus, a student who made a 49 on a test ended up with a 70 in the grade book (for those of you who went to government schools like me, that's the square root of 49 times ten).

This is what's happening at our 'best' schools. Don't believe me? Ask a college admissions worker how many students coming from our 'best' schools with grade point averages hovering near 4.0 need remediation when they get to college. It's an absolute joke. The overwhelming majority of children in our schools have a B average or above (mostly for self-esteem reasons), which serves to give them and their parents a false sense of achievement. It also results in people who 'feel really good' about their schools.

Please don't buy the lie. Your child's school is probably terrible. If you really care about the stewardship of your child's mind, don't send them back to the worst schools in the industrialized world.

3. America's Schools Are Morally Repugnant

The headlines speak for themselves. Student-teacher sex scandals, student-student sex, immodesty, foul language, drugs, alcohol, radical homosexual agendas, teachers taking students for abortions, "sexting" leading to suicide, sexually transmitted diseases, brutal beatings, and school shootings. These <u>are just some of the headlines</u> that have become the norm. And that does not include things like cheating, disrespect for authority, impropriety towards the opposite sex, and other moral behaviors children learn regularly and repeatedly in school.

Van Til said it better than I ever could: "non-Christian education puts the child in a vacuum…. The result is that child dies. Christian education alone really nurtures personality because it alone gives the child air and food…. Modern educational philosophy gruesomely insults our God and our Christ. How, then, do you expect to build anything positively Christian or theistic upon a foundation that negates Christianity and theism?…. No teaching of any sort is possible except in Christian schools."

Moreover, the system itself is funded by virtual theft. Homeowners are forced under threat of the loss of their property to pay for the education of other people's children. How is that appropriate? The government tells everyone that they have to send their children to school, then tells homeowners that they are going to be the ones to foot the bill whether they like it or not. Not only is this a form of welfare, it is also a form of theft.

For those of you ready to read me the riot act and yell and scream about paying for roads and bridges, hold on a minute. Why is it that we get all up-in-arms about our tax dollars being used to fund abortions (while our opponents make the roads and bridges argument), but we don't see this one? Our schools are morally repugnant.

They are also neo-Marxist, secular humanist indoctrination centers. Why should I as a Christian be forced to pay for children to have every vestige of Christianity beaten out of them? Americans are not forced to pay for Mormon schools, or Muslim schools; why should we be forced to pay for neo-Marxist schools (remember, all education is religious in nature)?

 Why should any Christian contribute to such a system by sending their children to such schools at the expense of others? And before you yell, "I'm just using the tax dollars I spent," ask yourself if you're willing to take advantage of all that abortion funding going to Planned Parenthood or those tax dollars going toward fetal stem cell research.

2. Government Education is Anti-Christian

"I am as sure as I am of Christ's reign that a comprehensive and centralized system of national education, separated from religion, as is now commonly proposed, will prove the most appalling enginery for the propagation of anti-Christian and atheistic unbelief, and of anti-social nihilistic ethics, individual, social and political, which this sin-rent world has ever seen." (A.A. Hodge)

Jesus made it quite clear when he said, **"Whoever is not with me is against me, and whoever does not gather with me scatters." (Matthew 12:30 ESV).** I am amazed at how many Christians refuse to acknowledge this fact as it relates to the government school system. Our education is either based on biblical truth, or some other 'alleged truth.' There is no such thing as neutrality in this regard.

All education is religious in nature. Since it is illegal for students in our government schools to be taught from a Christian perspective, then it follows that they must be taught from a non (or anti) Christian perspective.

As Hodge pointed out, the result of non-Christian education is anti-Christian education. Therefore, government schools must be anti-Christian. They can be nothing else. Therefore, to send a child to a government school is to have them trained in an anti-Christian environment for 14,000 instructional hours. To get that much instruction from church a child would have to attend two hours a week for one hundred and forty years!

1. The Bible Commands Christ-Centered Education

"This whole process of education is to be religious, and not only religious but Christian…. And as Christianity is the only true religion, and God in Christ the only true God, the only possible means of profitable education is the nurture and admonition of the Lord." (Charles Hodge)

I recognize that educational antinomianism is the norm in the modern American church. According to the common refrain, "It doesn't matter what educational choice you make… you just have to pray about it and do what the Lord leads your family to do." However, I must confess I find this concept disturbing on several fronts.

First, this kind of thinking denies the sufficiency of Scripture. The Bible speaks either directly or principally to every aspect of life.

THE WICKEDNESS OF PUBLIC EDUCATION

There are no grey areas. Sure, there are difficulties to discern, but education is not one of them. Though you won't find the word 'education' in Strong's Exhaustive Concordance, there are several passages that speak directly to the issue of training ourselves and our children intellectually, spiritually, philosophically and morally (See Deut. 6:6,7; Prov. 1:7; Eph. 6:4, etc). We also have numerous warnings against allowing others to influence us intellectually, spiritually, philosophically, and morally (Psalm 1; Rom. 12:1,2; 2 Cor. 6:14ff; Col. 2:8, etc.).

Second, this line of reasoning smacks of mysticism. Instead of making an argument with an open Bible we dismiss all opposition with the flippant, trite, overused, and theologically problem-laden phrase, "we prayed about it and this is what the Lord told us to do."

The Lord 'has spoken.' (Heb. 1:1-2) We are not awaiting new revelation. Instead of doing what the Lord 'told us,' Christians are commanded to do what the Lord 'has told us' in His Word.

The London Baptist Confession speaks to this matter rather poignantly: "The Holy Scripture is the only sufficient, certain, and infallible rule of all saving knowledge, faith and obedience; Although the light of Nature, and the works of creation and providence do so far manifest the goodness, wisdom and power of God, as to leave men inexcusable [sic.]; yet are they not sufficient to give that knowledge of God and His will, which is necessary unto salvation.

Therefore it pleased the Lord at sundry times, and in divers manners, to reveal Himself, and to declare His will unto His Church; and afterward for the better preserving, and propagating of the truth, and for the more sure establishment, and comfort of the

Church against the corruption of the flesh, and the malice of Satan, and of the World, to commit the same wholly unto writing; which makes the Holy Scriptures to be most necessary, those former ways of Gods revealing His will unto His people being now ceased."

The Cambridge Declaration states: "We reaffirm the inerrant Scripture to be the sole source of written divine revelation, which alone can bind the conscience. The Bible alone teaches all that is necessary for our salvation from sin and is the standard by which all Christian behavior must be measured. We deny that any creed, council or individual may bind a Christian's conscience, that the Holy Spirit speaks independently of or contrary to what is set forth in the Bible, or that personal spiritual experience [i.e., "the Lord told me"] can ever be a vehicle of revelation."

There's enough here for an entire series of posts (so many posts… so little time), but for now let me simply say that the "the Lord told me" line of argumentation has serious theological problems. We must make our educational decisions with an open Bible. "The Lord told me" is no substitute for 'the Bible says!' Please don't make a decision about your child's education without consulting (and obeying) the Scriptures.

Conclusion

How I long for voices like Hodge, Van Til, and Machen (who called government education a "soul-killing system") to be heard among my Christian brethren. However, with over eighty-five percent of our children in the government schools and more government schoolteachers and administrators than any other 'denomination,' it is highly unlikely that our side will prevail on this issue any time soon.

THE WICKEDNESS OF PUBLIC EDUCATION

One wonders what the schools will have to do to our children before we are willing to acknowledge the folly of our choices. In the meantime, I will continue to watch, fight, and pray, and try to convince as many of you as I can to liberate your children from Caesar's indoctrination camps.

Voddie Baucham is a husband, father, pastor, author, professor, conference speaker and church planter.

CHAPTER NINE

The Dangers of Critical Race Theory

Nation's Largest Teachers' Union Resolves to Promote Critical Race Theory

The National Education Association (NEA) has moved to openly promote the teaching of Critical Race Theory (CRT) in K-12 schools and to oppose any bans on instruction in both the Marxist ideology and the widely discredited New York Times' "1619 Project."

During its virtual representative assembly, held June 30-July 3, the nation's largest teachers' union agreed to "research the organizations attacking educators," doing what it referred to as "anti-racist work."

As well as to "use the research already done and put together a list of resources and recommendations for state affiliates, locals, and individual educators to utilize when they are attacked."

THE WICKEDNESS OF PUBLIC EDUCATION

The attacks on anti-racist teachers are increasing, coordinated by well-funded organizations such as the Heritage Foundation. We need to be better prepared to respond to these attacks so that our members can continue this important work.

NEA also adopted New Business Item 39, a measure that vows to "share and publicize, through existing channels, information already available on critical race theory (CRT) – what it is and what it is not." The union's resolution plans to have "a team of staffers for members who want to learn more and fight back against anti-CRT rhetoric."

NEA intends to "join with Black Lives Matter at School and the Zinn Education Project to call for a rally this year on October 14 – George Floyd's birthday – as a national day of action to teach lessons about structural racism and oppression."

The union added:

The Association will further convey that in teaching these topics, it is reasonable and appropriate for the curriculum to be informed by academic frameworks for understanding and interpreting the impact of the past on current society, including critical race theory.

The NEA's resolutions have undercut the left's narrative that CRT is not being taught in K-12 schools, as Fox News reported Saturday.

Parents across the country are swarming school board meetings, demanding that schools end the teaching of the principles of CRT, which embraces the concept that all American institutions are systemically racist, with whites as oppressors and blacks as victims. However, many school superintendents and board members have denied they are teaching CRT concepts in response to parents' and students' outrage.

*Remember, all communists are liars. Study the horrors of communism in countries like Russia, Cuba, Venezuela, China etc. Not only are they liars, but they are mass murderers, rapists, pedophiles, and oppressors of the masses, haters of freedom. – Doc Yeager

In Guilford, Connecticut, for example, Fox 61 News observed superintendent Dr. Paul Freeman denied his district is teaching CRT: Dr. Paul Freeman says it is inaccurate that this is being taught in schools. In a statement, he said in part:

"We are working in Guilford Schools to be more equitable in our practice, to embrace diverse texts in our classrooms, to diversify our teaching ranks, to address difficult historical events honestly and openly, and to ensure that all children feel heard in their schools." (Please notice the doubletalk)

A similar statement was made by Jeff Porter, superintendent of the Cumberland-North Yarmouth, Maine, school district.

Breitbart News reported:

Porter denied his district uses Critical Race Theory (CRT). However, following the death of George Floyd, the district sent a letter to the community, expressing its "solidarity with Black Movement leaders" and detailing its decision to work with Community Change Inc. (CCI), a Boston-based company that self-describes on Twitter as "a non-profit that challenges systemic racism with a special focus on white people."

"Can't dismantle white supremacy without dismantling

THE WICKEDNESS OF PUBLIC EDUCATION

capitalism," CCI states.

NEA's adoption of the resolutions will commit President Becky Pringle "to make public statements across all lines of media that support racial honesty in education including but not limited to critical race theory."

The union plans to invest an additional $127,600 to carry out its plan to openly publicize CRT and another $56,500 to conduct research on critics of CRT and obstruct their efforts.

Nearly half of all states in the United States are taking steps to prohibit the teaching of CRT and its concepts.

QUOTES ON PUBLIC EDGUCATION

"It isn't a coincidence that governments everywhere want to educate children. Government education, in turn, is supposed to be evidence of the state's goodness and its concern for our well-being. The real explanation is less flattering. If the government's propaganda can take root as children grow up, those kids will be no threat to the state apparatus. They'll fasten the chains to their own ankles."
— Llewellyn H. Rockwell Jr.

"With modern technology, it is the easiest of tasks for a media, guided by a narrow group of political manipulators, to speak constantly of democracy and freedom while urging regime changes everywhere on earth but at home. A curious condition of a republic based roughly on the original Roman model is that it cannot allow true political parties to share in the government. What then is a true political party: one that is based firmly in the interest of a class be

it, workers or fox hunters. Officially we have two parties which are in fact wings of a common party of property with two right wings. Corporate wealth finances each. Since the property party controls every aspect of media they have had decades to create a false reality for a citizenry largely uneducated by public schools that teach conformity with an occasionally advanced degree in consumerism."
— Gore Vidal

"It constantly amazes me that defenders of the free market are expected to offer certainty and perfection while the government has only to make promises and express good intentions. Many times, for instance, I've heard people say, "A free market in education is a bad idea because some child somewhere might fall through the cracks," even though in today's government school, millions of children are falling through the cracks every day."
— Lawrence W. Reed

"The free school is the promoter of that intelligence which is to preserve us as a free nation. Suppose we are to have another contest in the near future of our national existence. In that case, I predict that the dividing line will not be Mason and Dixon's, but between patriotism and intelligence on the one side—and superstition, ambition, and ignorance on the other."
— Ulysses S. Grant

"History has been stolen from us and replaced with guilt-inducing lies."
— Stefan Molyneux

"Trust in families and in neighborhoods and individuals to make sense of the important question, 'What is education for?' If some of them answer differently from what you might prefer, that's really

not your business, and it shouldn't be your problem. Our type of schooling has deliberately concealed the fact that such a question must be framed and not taken for granted if anything beyond a mockery of democracy is to be nurtured. It is illegitimate to have an expert answer that question for you."
— John Taylor Gatto, Dumbing Us Down: The Hidden Curriculum of Compulsory Schooling

---

"In brief, the teaching process, as commonly observed, has nothing to do with the investigation and establishment of facts, assuming that actual facts may ever be determined. Its sole purpose is to cram the pupils, as rapidly and as painlessly as possible, with the largest conceivable outfit of current axioms, in all departments of human thought—to make the pupil a good citizen, which is to say, a citizen differing as little as possible, in positive knowledge and habits of mind, from all other citizens.

In other words, it is the mission of the pedagogue, not to make his pupils think, but to make them think right, and the more nearly his own mind pulsates with the great ebbs and flows of popular delusion and emotion, the more admirably he performs his function. He may be an ass, but this is surely no demerit in a man paid to make asses of his customers."
— H.L. Mencken, A Mencken Chrestomathy

"Doesn't anything socialistic make you want to throw up? Like great public schools, or health insurance for all?"
— Kurt Vonnegut, A Man Without a Country

"It's as if every classroom has its own pied piper luring children away from their parents, from their own desires—from whatever they'd known to be true before entering that school building. Who gave them the right to access our minds? Why did they think they

had that authority? We were innocent children!"
— Philip Wyeth, Reparations Mind

Six Reasons You Should Get Your Kids Out of Public Schools

By Zachary Garris

Let me make a bold statement—Christian parents still willing to send their children to public school are either ignorant or in denial. I am willing to give most people the benefit of the doubt and assume they are in denial. What are they in denial of? The fact that American public schools train children in an atheistic worldview and indoctrinate them with a leftist agenda.

"But my school is different," you say. Is it really?

Consider the following. Every American public school is subject to Supreme Court rulings that have banned the Bible, prayer, and the teaching of creationism. In other words, every American public school is forced to teach a secular worldview (or, more accurately, an atheistic worldview). Some public schools may have more Christian teachers than others. But this does not matter, as they cannot legally teach as Christians. Their Christian worldview is not allowed in the classroom.

Even if your local school objects, it does not have much control. Each school is at the mercy of its state, which controls curriculum and the teacher certification process. Today, most states dumb down the humanities, and then they restrict the pool of teachers to those who have attended leftist colleges of education.

So no, your public school is not any different from the rest.

THE WICKEDNESS OF PUBLIC EDUCATION

Six Reasons to Abandon Public Schools

I would like to draw this out more by providing six reasons why you should get your kids out of public school. Whether you are ignorant of what is going on or are just in denial of the situation, these points should help move you to reconsider the government schools and look into alternative options.

#1 Public schools teach an atheistic worldview.

In fact, they are legally bound to do so. The Supreme Court banned prayer in Engel v. Vitale (1962) and Bible reading in Abington School District v. Schempp (1963). The schools are therefore not "neutral" but rather anti-Christian. The most obvious example is that they teach that humans came about through the natural means of Darwinian evolution rather than God's creative work. You can respond that some courses like math are more objective and thus not as harmful.

This is true. However, the math teacher who ignores God is still training children to think apart from God and His Word. And math is not the only subject taught in school. Children who attend public schools sit under unbelieving instruction for 30-plus hours per week. This has an impact on children.

#2 Public schools undermine Christian morality.

All education is moral. But since they have banned God's Word, public schools have had to look elsewhere for moral instruction. They have replaced the Ten Commandments with moral relativism—unless, of course, you are unwilling to accept something on the leftist agenda (like embracing LGBTQ). If you

137

object, then they call you a bigot. Furthermore, they push promiscuity in their sex education courses.

#3 Public schools neglect Western Christian history and thought.

This should be obvious. Western civilization and American history are too Christian (and too white!). So the public schools have decided to ignore all of that. No more church history, Western classics, or even logic. Even American history is whitewashed. So now they have "social studies," whatever that means.

#4 Public schools slant American history, government, and economics in favor of the state.

Western societies have traditionally esteemed both liberty and responsibility. But these virtues get in the way of big government and hefty politician salaries. So the bureaucrats have decided to do away with these virtues. Instead, they have decided to redesign school curriculum, use leftist textbooks, and train teachers in leftist universities—all to slant the humanities in favor of statism. The public schools have undoubtedly contributed to the growing popular endorsement of the welfare state and its usurpation of the role of parents (in education) and the church (in charity). It is no coincidence that the size of the state has grown along with the rise of the government school system.

#5 Public schools expose kids to bad influences.

As if the content in the classroom is not bad enough, public schools are filled with drugs, violence, and sexual immorality. Homeschoolers are always accused of being poorly "socialized." But critics leave out the fact that much of the "socialization" that takes place in public schools is entirely undesirable. Parents should seek to protect children and provide them with a safe and healthy upbringing.

*From the author: your children are being traumatized by insane and immoral indoctrination in the public school system. They no longer can trust who they are or what they are by simply looking in the mirror when they step out of the shower. They are being put into a confusing position of deciding what sex they are by being told they can not believe their own eyes. That is pure insanity and demonic to the core. – Doc Yeager

#6 Worst of all, public schools accomplish all of this through force.

It is bad enough that the government schools are anti-Christian. But what makes them so evil is their reliance on force through compulsory attendance laws and confiscatory taxation. Thankfully, parents in every state can opt-out of the system by providing alternative education. However, no one can opt-out of the taxes.

We are all forced to pay for the public school system, even if we do not use it. The government thus steals our money and forces parents who opt-out to pay double tuition. Poor parents are unable to opt-out, and middle-class families often cave to the financial pressure and send their kids there even if they have serious concerns. The public schools, therefore, undermine the authority and responsibility of the family.

This last point is so important. No one would be making a big deal of a private school that taught a leftist, atheistic worldview. Why? Because attendance and funding would be entirely voluntary. No one would be required to pay for such a school except the parents who wish to send their children there.

This is the exact opposite of how public schools work. They use compulsion to fuel the system, thus infringing upon the rights of citizens. Education belongs to the family, not the state. Education should therefore be provided in private institutions that are entirely voluntary. Government schools monopolize the market through coercion, making the schools inefficient and hurting the prospects of competition. This is why we pay so much in taxes towards public schools (often around 40% of local and state taxes). And it is why private Christian schools struggle so much to make it financially.

Such a powerful school system is an even greater danger when it is secularized, as in the case of America's public schools. The system has tons of money and the majority of students indoctrinates them into atheism. Is it any wonder that America has become so progressive since the state school system went into full force in the late-1800s?

Christian Resistance

It sounds great to try to reform the public school system. However, you cannot reform something that is corrupt at it is a very root. The root problem must be addressed—and that problem is that the public schools are controlled by the government. The government forces people to attend and pay for their schools. This means the only solution is to abandon the government school system. What we need is a privatized system. Reform is a bad idea.

Many parents know that the public schools are not the best option. But they hope that as parents, they can also influence their children, correcting things taught during the day and filling in the gaps of things left out. But is this a realistic goal? This places a difficult, if not impossible, burden on parents.

And why would any parent want to unnecessarily expose his or her children to such harmful "education"? This is particularly a good question when there are great alternative options, including homeschooling and private schooling. Children who attend public school are not only being exposed to evil but are missing out on the great Christian education they could be receiving. They could be studying logic, Western civilization, church history, Bible, and classic literature, along with math and science—from a biblical perspective.

God commands His people to train their children **"in the discipline and instruction of the Lord" (Ephesians 6:4).** It is hard to understand how anyone who knows what is going on in the public schools can still think they aid in this task.

HOME SCHOOLING SAVED OUR CHILDRENS SOULS

Carl Rutherford - 18 Years ago, the lord led my wife to home school our children. The United Kingdom school system was not that bad back then as it is now and at first my answer was NO. However, a few days later God got on my case, and said to me "if I have put this in your wife's heart who are you to not support her".

Immediately I saw the log in my own eye, and how it was my responsibility to get behind her and support her. I told her I could not do it myself as I have not the ability, but I will support you 100%. I also warned her that I would soon "get it in the neck" for doing this.

Well very soon after this, within weeks, the dark clouds came and our families from both sides, Christian & non-, came against us. Most of the brothers and sister in the faith that we knew at that time all questioning our integrity in this decision, my parents were also far from impressed, but the scripture were made clear to us and it was really and easy decision after the light had come in.

Proverbs 17:6 Children's children are the crown of old men; and the glory of children are their fathers.

Proverbs 22:6Train up a child in the way he should go: and when he is old, he will not depart from it.

Proverbs 22:15Foolishness is bound in the heart of a child; but the rod of correction shall drive it far from him.

Proverbs 23:13Withhold not correction from the child: for if thou beatest him with the rod, he shall not die.

Proverbs 23:24The father of the righteous shall greatly rejoice: and he that begetteth a wise child shall have joy of him.

Looking back over the years at the great struggles in homeschooling in many areas I can see the wisdom of God and how blessed I am that I was not to proud to ignore God's voice and ways. Today the UK schooling is in dire issues, something I never foresaw happening. Today my 5 sons are growing beautifully and are very different to most children their ages, thank God. My wife has poured her heart into them, and has read the Psalms to them at bedtime, every night for years and years.

THE WICKEDNESS OF PUBLIC EDUCATION

Today's UK school system is in a dire mess, and so are the UK youth, who are struggling terribly with many things they have learned in school or universities. It will take a mighty move of God to win them back to the truth. Without a touch of God, this generation and the one below them will struggle Immensely.

There were times we were at our wits end with the continuous onslaught from brothers and sister in the faith and family, that continued to come to our door to attack us and only one thing kept us going throughout the years, when everybody we met disagreed with our stance, and I mean everybody.... except this....

Now and again, we would go out for a coffee & cake and every time we did, the spirit of God would bring a stranger to us. Each time these people we never knew or never seen again, would just come up to us and say....

" I just like to say how wonderful behaved your children are, they are wonderful and a real credit to you"

And with that they be gone. That happened so many times I cannot count the number, and each time the same words were spoken to us, and we saw that God was bringing people to us to encourage us on our path and keep us going in the way.

I know this without any doubt, that when your brother or sister fails to encourage you in the way of righteousness or in what God has laid on your heart, he will bring another to stimulate that which he started, so that you finish that which he began, Selah...

"If you miss that unction of the spirit in where he is leading you it will cost you dearly"

FROM THE AUTHORS PERSONAL LIFE

Dad Was Catholic my Mother Was Lutheran

Both my parents came from opposite religious backgrounds. He was Catholic and she was Lutheran. Personally, I do not think neither my father nor my mother were serious about their religious heritage. I know that my father wanted to be married in the Catholic Church, but because he had been married previously (even though it was only for three months) the priest would not perform the ceremony.

I do not know if a Lutheran minister or maybe just a justice of the peace did the ceremony. Even though my father sent us to a Catholic school and to Catholic Mass, I have never seen either one of my parents enter a church facility. However, we did pray a traditional Catholic prayer before every meal. My father prayed this prayer in the beginning. Later on, it was taken over by the oldest of the children who were still living at home.

Bless us, O Lord, and these Thy gifts, which we are about to receive from Thy bounty, through Christ our Lord. Amen.

Catholic school education

When we moved to Mukwonago my father placed my brother and my sister into the Catholic school of the St James Catholic Parish. In those days it was a simple one room schoolhouse right across from the main sanctuary.

Eventually they built a brand-new facility which I attended until the end of my third grade. I believe all of us were placed into the public school system in 1964. This was because my father was not keeping his financial responsibility the way that the church required it. As a result, the priest informed my family that we were no longer welcomed to attend the school.

We still did attend the church that is my brother, sister and I, until I joined the military. Of course, our attendance was very erratic. Many times we would simply go to Christmas mass or sunrise Easter service. I still remember him with the letter in his hand informing us as an eight-year-old boy.

St. James Parish is still in operation to this day at 830 County Rd NN Mukwonago, WI 53149

Held Back a Grade

I attended kindergarten when I was five years old, but I was a very slow learner. They had to hold me back for another year just for me to get the basics.

It wasn't too difficult because even though I was six years old in kindergarten class, you did not really feel the pressure because of being in a one-room schoolhouse. I think that in that one room school house there was about 40 to 50 of us. In the basement of that old schoolhouse was where the teenagers were located.

Beating My Head on the Hardwood Floor

One of the most painful things I can remember as being a young child was my constant fight with the pressure in my head from my eardrums.

I was constantly at the doctors, and they were trying different things in order to relieve this pressure. In those days it was not yet practiced putting tubes into the inner years.

Do ear tubes relieve pressure?
Once inside the ear, these tubes will: Reduce pressure. ... Ear tubes allow air to enter the ear, equalizing the pressure between the inner ear and the outside world. This eases pain and helps prevent accumulation of liquid in the middle ear. May 2, 2017

My mother would hold me, and at times she would take the cigarette smoke from her mouth and blow it into my ears. I remember many times having to stay at home because of my ear problems. My parents worked, my mother as a waitress, and my father in Waukesha, Wisconsin as an electronics expert.

I would find myself at home alone with so much pain in my head that I would get desperate. In our small dining room, we had a hardwood floor. To this day, I remember crying on my hands and knees and banging my head hard against the floor. Yes, hitting my head against the floor hurt, but it seemed to relieve some of the pressure from my inner ears.

.

CHAPTER TEN
AUTHORS PERSONAL STORY CONTINUES

Mocked As a Child Because of My Speech

My speech was so bad that very few people could understand me. Many times, my sister Debbie would speak for me. I could not speak in a way that people could understand me, but because my hearing was so difficult, I often did not know what people were saying.

People would ask me a question that many times I would just stare at them. That's when my sister Debbie would jump in to try to bring about some kind of understanding. From the first time I went to school until I left when I was 15 years old, I was constantly ridiculed about my speech. They would imitate me, slurring their words. Instead of saying car it sounded like Cow. When it came to rolling my tongue or pronouncing the R sound correctly, it seemed to be completely impassable. When God finally healed my hearing and my speech it brought about a drastic change in how people treated me.

Speech Therapist with Big Lips

Even though I was attending a Catholic school, a speech therapist was made available to me at the local public school. So through the week, I would be transported to the public school for this lady to work with me. Now, I was between 5 to 7 years old during those years that they were trying to help me to speak better.

I do remember that she was a beautiful teacher who probably from my recollections in her mid-30s. She was always kind and gentle to me. The number one thing I remember about her was her lips. I can still see her lips. She would have me sit at a table with her right across from her. It must've been a slender table because she seemed to have her lips very close to my face. She would tell me to imitate the movements of her tongue and her lips.

My greatest challenge was to move my tongue in a sufficient way to form the words properly. I still remember her over and over trying to get me to roll my tongue. To say car instead of Cow. To say Yeager instead of Yeaga. Yes, I could not even say my own last name. The children would mock me by saying my name the way that I did. Children can be very cruel at times.

THE WICKEDNESS OF PUBLIC EDUCATION

Sad to say, I'm not convinced that all of that speech therapy helped me very much. I kept my mouth shut until 1975; in about March I was touched of God while in prayer, baptized in the Holy Ghost. When kneeling next to my bunk in the Navy, God completely took away this speech impediment. Since then, I had been trying to make up for what I lost for the first 19 years of my life.

<hr>

Transferred to the Public School
Clarendon Avenue Elementary

In the fourth grade, my parents had to transfer me to the Clarendon Avenue Elementary. If I correctly understand, St. James Catholic School would not allow us to continue to attend. I know it had something to do with money. Not quite sure if it's because my dad did not donate to the church or could not meet the cost of the tuition.

This was a very emotional and drastic event in my life. At least in the Catholic school, the nuns did everything they could to stop students from intimidating each other or making fun of each other.

Now I had stepped into an environment where I felt like I was surrounded by nothing but cannibalistic children. Because of my hearing problems and my speech impediment, the harassment was endless. This caused me to withdraw even more into a shell. Also, the public school system brought my brother Dennis and my sister Debbie into the drug world. Debbie was three grades ahead of me, and Dennis was four grades.

Their introduction to the public school system was the junior high school and high school students. This constant harassment

149

eventually caused me to leave school when I was 15 years old, right before my 16th birthday.

Beat Up by Tim Frost

It was my first year in the public school system, and I was experiencing a very difficult time. One day I was walking across the blacktop playground with my arms full of books. The next thing I knew, there was somebody that was off to my right. Before I knew what hit me, a fist slammed into my face. I was so shocked that I dropped all of my books.

There standing in front of me, was the school bully. Tim Frost by name. He punched me a couple more times in the face before I knew what was happening. I had no idea why he was beating me up. A bunch of kids came running, and they encouraged him to keep pounding on me. I remember to this day standing there and almost weeping. I did not know what to do at that moment. In the Catholic school, we never had fights.

When I did not respond to his punches, eventually, he walked away just laughing at me. All the kids were laughing at me. I'm not even entirely sure if my parents ever knew what happened. But from that moment forward, I began to progressively nosedive mentally and emotionally.

My family had already been a mess because of my dad's drinking, and my mom being sick all the time. From 11 years old up and to my 19th birthday, it seemed like I was living in the twilight zone. Yet God was able to keep me during those years when I should've been dead from suicidal tendencies and stupidity.

THE WICKEDNESS OF PUBLIC EDUCATION

Dennis Gets His Two Front Teeth Knocked out

As I wrote earlier, when we ended up in the public school, my brother and sister and I ran into a complete mess. My brother Dennis began to run with the wrong crowd. Now, my brother had knocked out my front tooth a number of years before this incident.

Possibly what happened to him is simply the fact that he was reaping what he sowed. I do not believe for a moment that everything that happens is the will of God. I know that is a complete lie. We are dealing with a demonic world, plus we have the power to make our own choices.

Dennis was out one Friday night when he was about 16 years old. He and some of his buddies were looking to rumble. Well, they ran into a guy who probably was about three years older than Dennis. He got into a fight with my brother Dennis, and with one punch, this guy with his fist clipped off my brother's two front teeth like they were nothing.

The guy felt so bad about what he did that he put my brothers' bike in the back of his pickup truck. And then he brought him home. I still remember watching him take my brother's bike out of the pickup truck. Dennis turned around and looked at me. He seemed like he was trying to smile, it could be that his mouth was simply hurting. Right there in front of me, I saw his two front top teeth were missing.

Don't Mess with Me

I ended up in junior high school, and when I had been in the fourth grade, there had been a kid by the name of Tim Frost, who was a bully. The first year I was in public school, he had surprised me. He punched me in the face, causing me to drop all of my books and to break out crying while the kids laughed at me. So here it was approximately three years later.

I was coming down the hallway, and Tim Frost was with two of his friends. I was coming down the middle of the hallway.

Now, all the children would go either to the left or the right to avoid these three Bully's, but I was in a nasty mood on that day. So I walked right down the middle of the hallway. When I got to Tim Frost, my shoulder slammed into his shoulder.

Immediately he tried to grab me, and I grabbed him, and we began to wrestle in the hallway. Well, the teachers began to come, so I told him that I would meet him out in the playground at the end of the day. So everybody was shocked that Mikey Yeager, who was considered by many to be retarded because I could not hear very well and had a terrible speech impediment, would challenge Tim Frost to a fight.

Well, at the end of the day, I was waiting for him, tucked up against the edge of the school building. I knew that he could beat me easily. The minute he went past me, I jumped out, and I wrapped my left arm around his neck and his head pulling him to the ground. When I got him to the ground I began to pummel him with my right fist.

Here come the kids and they all came to watch me and Tim roll across the ground as I punched him, and he punched me. This went on for quite a while until finally a teacher from the school came and broke up the fight. From that time forward, I never experienced another problem from any of the kids in the school. They must have figured that I was so mentally unstable that I was not someone that they wanted to mess with. So this was typical life in the public school system for me.

Educate Children by Starting a School

In 1986 as we were constructing our new church facility, the Lord spoke to me about having a **Christian** school K to 12. The Lord spoke to my heart the importance of raising up children in the way they should go!

Proverbs 22:6 Train up a child in the way he should go: and when he is old, he will not depart from it.

By **Faith** we stepped out and received a license from Pennsylvania to run a private **Christian** School! Till this date

(2020) we still have our license even though the school is not in operation at this moment!

Michael and Ritalin

In our church, we had several women that were teachers in the public school system. One of these ladies was extremely intelligent, and her husband was the electrician doing all our electrical work in the building.

She very much wanted to be involved in our **Christian** school, so it was agreed upon to hire her to become our principal. The only problem we discovered was that the secular world had greatly influenced her. So she began to try to run our **Christian** school based upon the public school system. Now, I am not speaking about the curriculum because we did have a good **Spirit**ual curriculum that we used in the school.

What I am talking about is how she looked upon the children. Now, my son Michael seemed to be a little bit hyperactive, which is normal for a young boy. When they get hyper, you simply need to keep them busy to use that energy for something constructive. My son Michael had ants in his pants, and so he needed to be challenged.

One day this lady called my wife and me into her office for a special meeting. She informed us that Michael needed to be put on Ritalin because of his hyperactivity.

Ritalin: This medication is used to treat attention deficit hyperactivity disorder - ADHD. It works by changing the amounts of certain natural substances in the brain. Side Effects - Nervousness, trouble sleeping, loss of appetite, weight loss, dizziness, nausea, vomiting, or headache may occur.

I did not argue with her or even discuss it with her. I just thanked her for her opinion and said my wife and I would pray about it. So we did pray about it and I knew in my heart that we would never put any of our children on any kind of mind-altering drugs.

We have not taken children into our school from that day forward unless the parents were willing to take them off of mind-altering drugs. We always had wonderful success with the parents who agreed to do this. We're not talking about medication that the physical body requires but drugs that affect the human mind or emotions. This simply opens the door for demonic activity.

We did not fire this sister from being the principal of our school, but she simply left on her own the next year. I know within my heart if we would have put Michael or any of our sons on Ritalin or any other mind-altering drugs, it would have destroyed their lives like so many other young men.

TRAIN UP A CHILD IN THE WAY HE
SHOULD GO; EVEN WHEN HE IS OLD
HE WILL NOT DEPART FROM IT.
PROVERBS 22:6

Gods Instructions on Raising Children

When I gave my heart to **Christ**, I entered a brand-new world that I never knew existed. As I read my Bible, I immediately recognized that I had to change much of my thinking and belief system. One of these areas was how to raise children.

When I first went to school, my parents sent me to a Catholic parochial school, but by the time I hit third grade, they could no longer afford to give me private education. This is when I stepped into a nightmare of the public education school system. I had several disadvantages. First, I had a speech impediment that was so bad you could barely understand what I was saying. For years, my sister Debbie, who was two years older than me, would tell people what I said.

The second major issue I had was with my hearing. I was born with immovable bones in my ears; therefore every time I got congested, tremendous pain would hit my head from the pressure. Because I could not hear very well, and people did not clearly understand what I was saying, I was considered to be mentally retarded. I went through terrible humiliation in public school to the point where I quit when I was 15.

When I was born again, I discovered that the Jewish boys stayed at their daddy side to learn their father's trade. Today we just go off to work and send our children somewhere else to educate them. I decided right then and there that if I was ever going to have any children, they would be at my side. That's how it was carried on through the generations of Abraham all the way up to the times of **Christ**.

My natural father drove it into my heart, and my brother's and sister's heart that we needed to leave home as soon as possible. My older brother and sister went when they were 18. I left home right after I was 17 years old to join the navy. If you look at the biblical standard from Abraham up through the old covenant, this was not the case. The Israelite families all stayed together through their whole lives. It was not forced upon the sons to stay, but most of them chose to stay.

Now, Peter, the apostle, was a fisherman because his daddy was a fisherman. His daddy before him was a fisherman. This is passed on from generation to generation. When I discovered this in the Bible I said within my heart; I will teach my boys to do what I do, for they can do it too. From the time they were little, my three sons and at times my daughter have always been at my side. If you go into our church, you will see five stone-built fireplaces. I taught my boys to lay those fireplaces. Most of the work done when it comes to the fireplaces in the church is from my sons.

I also introduced my boys to computer technology, radio station broadcasting, TV broadcasting, TV editing, writing, publishing books, and preaching the gospel. As a result, my four children have all either written books or are in the process of writing books.

I've had all my family since they were little out on the streets preaching and sharing the gospel with me. I used to take them into the rough-and-tumble parts of Baltimore and Philadelphia. They have preached the gospel and help feed the hungry for as long as they can remember. They are all preachers of the gospel. I did not force this upon them, I just simply had them at my side with their mother.

Daily we still gathered together to eat, talk, pray and worship together. My children are all free to come and go as God leads them and guides them. Through the years, they have come and gone. At the writing of this book they all live on the property of the church that I pastor. What a blessing they are to my wife and I and our congregation.

Psalm 127: 1 Except the Lord build the house, they labour in vain that build it: except the Lord keep the city, the watchman waketh but in vain.2 It is vain for you to rise up early, to sit up late, to eat the bread of sorrows: for so he giveth his beloved sleep.3 Lo, children are an heritage of the Lord: and the fruit of the womb is his reward.4 As arrows are in the hand of a mighty man; so are children of the youth.5 Happy is the man that hath his quiver full of them: they shall not be ashamed, but they shall speak with the enemies in the gate.

Deliverance of Sarah of Tourette syndrome

Tourette syndrome (TS) is a neurological disorder characterized by repetitive, stereotyped, involuntary movements and vocalizations called tics.

I am entirely convinced that it is a demonic affliction. How many would make the mistake of thinking that someone with this syndrome is demon-possessed, but they are oppressed! These demonic spirits come and go, just like many people who have seizures. This is not a one-time pronouncement of deliverance. This is a true story of one young lady who was delivered by a progressive application of spiritual truths and authority.

Three months before school was out in 1994, I received a phone call from a husband and wife from Carlisle, Pennsylvania.

THE WICKEDNESS OF PUBLIC EDUCATION

They called, asking if we could help them. They had been watching my TV program, which was aired on their local TV station. They knew from my messages on TV that we had a **Christ**ian school. In addition, they had a daughter who was ten years old, who desperately needed help. Not only did she have tics syndrome, but she had major emotional problems.

The principal of the public school that she attended was demanding they place her in to a mental institution. She was completely uncontrollable. Whenever they would try to discipline her, she would run from them, often ending up in the parking lot, crawling under the cars. One time when she was in the principal's office, Sarah got so angry that she completely wiped out this office.

They told me that she had gone completely berserk, trashing everything in her sight. The principal of the school could not handle it anymore. The only other option this couple had was to see if somebody would take her into their school. Our school was over 30 miles away from where they lived, but they were willing to drive it every day. I told them that I would pray about it to see what the Lord spoke to me. I truly felt in my heart that we could help this young lady. A meeting was set up to meet the parents with their daughter Sarah.

I always like to pray before I make any commitments. I sought the Lord about this terrible situation with their daughter. As I spoke face-to-face with the parents and met Sarah for the first time, I perceived in my heart we could help her. First I told them that if we were going to help Sarah for the next three months, they would have to allow us to do what we felt needed to be done.

The first thing they would need to do was take Sarah off all mind-altering drugs, which the public school had put her on. This is always one of our requirements for a child to come to our school. From 1985, up to this moment, in our school we never allowed any mind-altering drugs. In every situation, we have seen **GOD** do marvelous things in a student's life.

The second thing I told the parents is that we would want them not to hang around at all at the school once they drop their daughter off. I perceived by the spirit of **GOD** that a lot of Sarah's problem was that she was using her condition as a way to get attention from her mother and father. This proved to be correct because every time her mother came to pick her up, the tics became much worse. When she first came to our school, her head would shake back and forth very violently all day long. It was excruciating to watch.

I had a meeting with my teachers, informing them that they were not to lift their voices or yell at Sarah for any reason. We were not going to put her in a situation that would stir up the devils that were manifesting through her.

Many so-called **Christ**ians, especially the spirit-filled ones, would have been trying to cast the devils out of her the minute they saw her because they would have thought she was demon-possessed. Granted, there were devils at work, but she was not possessed. She was oppressed, depressed and at times obsessed. People who do not have a lot of wisdom immediately try to cast devils out without getting the mind of **CHRIST**.

The Spirit of **God** told me what we needed to do. Every morning when her mother dropped her off, I would take her with one of the school's female teachers into an office. I would speak very softly to Sarah, telling her that we would like to pray with her before the beginning of the day.

I would simply speak in a very soft voice over her that which was the will of **GOD**. This prayer would usually only be about five minutes long. Then I would tell her that she was going to have a wonderful day. Off to her class, she would go. We did not treat her any different than the other students. If they began to have problems with her throughout the day, they would send someone to get me.

Once again, we would take her into an office (with a lady teacher), and I would gently pray over her in the name of **JESUS CHRIST**. I also came against the demonic spirits that were causing the tics syndrome. I never got loud, authoritative, or weird. I would simply take authority over them in a quiet, gentle voice. Immediately there was a wonderful change in Sarah. Every day she was getting better. Not only did the tics syndrome cease eventually, but she became an A+ student. It was obvious to me at the beginning that Sarah was a brilliant girl who was not being challenged at the school she attended.

By the end of the three months, Sarah was completely free. She was a happy, smiling, hard-working A+ student. We could not have asked for a better young girl. I am sorry to say that we never saw Sarah or her parents again at the end of those three months. I guess they had gotten what they needed, and off they went. This is very typical in my experience.

When the next school year rolled around, I received a very strange phone call one day from the Carlisle school district. The principal was on the phone wanting to talk to me. When I got on the phone with this principal, who was a lady, she asked me a question with a tone of absolute surprise and wonder. She said to me: what in the world did you do with Sarah? She is completely changed!

I said to this principal, who was over a large school district, "What we did with Sarah you're not going to be able to do!" So I said to her: we began to pray over her very gently, every day, consistently in the name of **JESUS CHRIST**. You could hear a pin drop for the next couple of moments. The next thing I heard was, OH, okay, goodbye! The principal hung up the phone!

The public school system has no concept of these realities. They are antichrist in their approach and their education system. Little Sarah would have been sent to a psych ward where they would have drugged her even more to the day that she died.

Calvary Road and Revival

I came across a book that had a wonderful impact on my life called **"CALVARY ROAD"**! It is about a mighty revival that **GOD** brought in an overseas mission. This book is by Roy Hession, and it very simply outlines personal revival (sanctification) through being filled with the Holy Spirit. As it says in 2 Thessalonians 2:13, the work of the Holy Spirit in our life is to save us "through the sanctifying work of the Spirit and through belief in the truth."

Rom. 8:4 tells us that **"the righteous requirements of the law might be fully met in us, who do not live according to the sinful nature but according to the Spirit"**. In this little book, the process of sanctification, through surrendering all, is simply and clearly revealed for those who are willing to seek the Lord with all their heart.

I was so impressed and convicted by this little book that I ordered the book by the case. I took this book and distributed it to the whole congregation for free. I also gave this book to all our staff, including the teachers in our **Christ**ian school. We even gave this book to the older classes in our **Christ**ian school.

I began to preach along the line of repentance, prayer, and one hundred percent commitment to **JESUS CHRIST**; that there should be no hidden sin in our lives. The fire of **GOD** fell in our church. (Revival!) The Lord started working in such wonderful ways that the teenagers in our private school started weeping and crying in the classrooms.

We had to stop the classes when this happened. I walked into the sanctuary of the church one morning, and there were all the teenagers lying on the floor weeping, crying, and calling out to **GOD**! This wonderful move continued for a short season.

COME OUT FROM HER

2 Corinthians 6:17 Wherefore come out from among them, and be ye separate, saith the Lord, and touch not the unclean thing; and I will receive you.

Isaiah 52:11 Depart ye, depart ye, go ye out from thence, touch no unclean thing; go ye out of the midst of her; be ye clean, that bear the vessels of the Lord.

Revelation 18:4 And I heard another voice from heaven, saying, Come out of her, my people, that ye be not partakers of her sins, and that ye receive not of her plagues.

Acts 2:40And with many other words did he testify and exhort, saying, Save yourselves from this untoward generation.

Numbers 16:26And he spake unto the congregation, saying, Depart, I pray you, from the tents of these wicked men, and touch nothing of their's, lest ye be consumed in all their sins.

Proverbs 9:6 Forsake the foolish, and live; and go in the way of understanding.

Ezra 6:21 And the children of Israel, which were come again out of captivity, and all such as had separated themselves unto them from the filthiness of the heathen of the land, to seek the Lord God of Israel, did eat,

Jeremiah 51:6 Flee out of the midst of Babylon, and deliver every man his soul: be not cut off in her iniquity; for this is the time of the Lord's vengeance; he will render unto her a recompence.

How to Live in the Miraculous!

This is a quick explanation of how to live and move in the realm of the miraculous. Seeing divine interventions of **God** is not something that just spontaneously happens because you have been born-again. There are certain biblical principles and truths that must be evident in your life. This is a very basic list of some of these truths and laws:

1. You must give **Jesus Christ** your whole **HEART**. You cannot be lackadaisical in this endeavour. Being lukewarm in your walk with **God** is repulsive to the Lord. He wants 100% commitment.

Jesus gave His all, now it is our turn to give our all. He loved us 100%. Now we must love Him 100%.

My son, give me thine HEART, and let thine eyes observe my ways
(Proverbs 23:26).

So then because thou art lukewarm, and neither cold nor hot, I will spew thee out of my mouth (Revelation 3:16).

2. There must be a complete agreement with **God's Word**. We must be in harmony with the Lord in our attitude, actions, **Thoughts**, and deeds. Whatever the **Word** of **God** declares in the New Testament is what we whole**HEART**edly agree with.

Can two walk together, except they be agreed? (Amos 3:3).

For the eyes of the LORD run to and fro throughout the whole earth, to shew himself strong in the behalf of them whose HEART is perfect toward him (2 Chronicles 16:9).

3. Obey and do the **Word** from the **HEART**, from the simplest to the most complicated request or command. No matter what the **Word** says to do, do it! Here are some simple examples: Lift your hands in praise, in everything give thanks, forgive instantly, gather together with the saints, and give offerings to the Lord, and so on.

> *I can of mine own self do nothing: as I hear, I judge: and my judgment is just; because I seek not mine own will, but the will of the Father which hath sent me (John 5:30).*

4. Make **Jesus** the highest priority of your life. Everything you do, do not do it as unto men, but do it as unto **God**.

> *If ye then be risen with Christ, seek those things which are above, where Christ sitteth on the right hand of God. Set your affection on things above, not on things on the*

earth (Colossians 3:1-2).

5. Die to self! The old **Man** says, "My will be done!" The new **Man** says, "**God's** will be done!"

> *I am crucified with Christ: nevertheless I live; yet not I, but Christ liveth in me: and the life which I now live in the Flesh I live by the Faith of the Son of God, who loved me, and gave himself for me (Galatians 2:20).*

> *Now if we be dead with Christ, we believe that we shall also live with him (Romans 6:8).*

6. Repent the minute you get out of **God's** will—no matter how minor, or small the sin may seem.

Revelation 3:19 As many as I love, I rebuke and chasten: be zealous therefore, and repent.

7. Take one step at a time. **God** will test you (not to do evil) to see if you will obey him. *Whatever He tells you to do: by His **Word**, by His **Spirit**, or within your conscience, do it.* He will never tell you to do something contrary to His nature or His **Word**!

> *For whosoever shall do the will of my Father which is in heaven, the same is my brother, and sister, and mother (Matthew 12:50).*

ABOUT THE AUTHOR

Michael met and married his wonderful wife (Kathleen) in 1978. As a direct result of the Author and his wife's personal, amazing experiences with God, they have had the privilege to serve as pastors/apostles, missionaries, evangelist,

broadcasters, and authors for over four decades. By Gods Divine enablement's and Grace, Doc Yeager has written over 170 books, ministered over 10,000 Sermons, and having helped to start over 25 churches. His books are filled with hundreds of their amazing testimonies of Gods protection, provision, healing's, miracles, and answered prayers. They flow in the gifts of the Holy Spirit, teaching the Word of God, wonderful signs following and confirming God's Word. Websites Connected to Doc Yeager.

www.jilmi.org

www.wbntv.org

Some of the Books Written by Doc Yeager:
"Living in the Realm of the Miraculous – "1 to 5 "
"I need God Cause I'm Stupid"
"The Miracles of Smith Wigglesworth"
"How Faith Comes 28 WAYS"
"Horrors of Hell, Splendors of Heaven"
"The Coming Great Awakening"
"Sinners in The Hands of an Angry GOD",
"Brain Parasite Epidemic"
"My JOURNEY to HELL" - illustrated for teenagers
"Divine Revelation of Jesus Christ"
"My Daily Meditations"
"Holy Bible of JESUS CHRIST"
"War In The Heavenlies - (Chronicles of Micah)"
"My Legal Rights to Witness"
"Why We (MUST) Gather! - 30 Biblical Reasons"
"My Incredible, Supernatural, Divine Experiences"
"How GOD Leads & Guides! - 20 Ways"

"Weapons of Our Warfare"
"How You Can Be Healed"
"Hell Is For Real"
"Heaven Is For Real"
"God Still Heals"
"God Still Provides"
"God Still Protects"
"God Still Gives Dreams & Visions"
"God Still Does Miracles"
"God Still Gives Prophetic Words"
"Life Changing Quotes of Smith Wigglesworth"

Made in the USA
Middletown, DE
25 January 2023

21888788R00099